The Tablet of
the Holy Mariner

The Tablet of the Holy Mariner

An Illustrated Guide to Bahá'u'lláh's Mystical Writing in the Sufi Tradition

MICHAEL SOURS

KALIMÁT PRESS
LOS ANGELES

Text Copyright © 2002 by Michael Sours
Illustrations © 2002 by Michael Sours
All Rights Reserved.
Manufactured in the United States of America.

First Edition.

No part of this book may be reproduced in any manner without the express written consent of the publisher, except in the case of brief excerpts in critical reviews and articles. All inquiries should be addressed to Kalimát Press, 1600 Sawtelle Boulevard, Suite 310, Los Angeles, California, 90025.
www.kalimat.com
kalimatp@aol.com

Book design and composition by
Rohani Design, www.rohanidesign.com

Library of Congress Cataloging-in-Publication Data

Bahá'u'lláh, 1817–1892.
   [Lawh-i mallah al-quds. English]
   The tablet of the holy mariner ; an illustrated guide to Bahá'u'lláh's mystical writing in the sufi tradition / Michael Sours
      p. cm.
   Includes bibliographical references.
   ISBN 1-890688-19-3
   1. Bahai Faith—Doctrines. 2. Sufism. I. Sours, Michael II. Title.

BP362 .B34 2002
297.9'382—dc21   2001038542

To Mojgan

Contents

Preface   ix

———

The Tablet of the Holy Mariner   1

———

1. The authorship and date of the tablet   23

2. The literary style of the tablet   27

3. The interpretation of the tablet   33

4. The symbolism in the tablet   43

5. Reflections on the tablet: a verse-by-verse analysis   65

Notes   81

Bibliography   95

Preface

Sacred books and writings that reveal the divine mysteries and which exist to enable seekers to draw closer to the presence of God are in a category wholly separate from and incomparable to all other literary works. Nevertheless, the world's heritage of spiritual and sacred books include what are simultaneously recognized as some of the greatest works of literature. Referring to one of Bahá'u'lláh's books, the literary scholar Jan Rypka wrote that it "belongs rather to the realm of literature than to that of theology."[1] While many admirers of Bahá'u'lláh's theology would disagree with this assessment, Rypka's statement does suggest that even a person who fails to appreciate the spiritual depth of Bahá'u'lláh's writings, may nonetheless recognize their great literary quality.

The Tablet of the Holy Mariner is a small work in a large body of writings by Bahá'u'lláh, much of which remain untranslated from the Arabic and Persian originals. At the time this short Tablet was written in the second half of the nineteenth century, Bahá'u'lláh was known as a saint and leading personality in the remaining remnant of the persecuted Bábí religious community. His writings were an important source of inspiration to that community. In the years ahead, they would come to be regarded as sacred revelation by his followers, the Bahá'ís. However, Bahá'u'lláh's writings have an appeal that goes beyond the Bahá'í community. This is certainly evident in the Tablet of the Holy Mariner. The purpose of this book is to help introduce this particular Tablet to a wider audience. Those familiar with literature written by the great poets and mystics, especially the Sufi poets of the Islamic world, will find much that is familiar in this Tablet as well as much that is unique and new. The Tablet uses symbols common to the Sufi mystical tradition to create a vision of our inner spiritual universe—a cosmological order and stage on which Bahá'u'lláh unfolds a spiritual drama intended to help seekers overcome the greatest obstacles they face in the path to the divine Presence.

This book begins with a full translation of the Tablet accompanied with narrative illustrations. These original illustrations were created specifically for the Tablet and are based on the symbolism observed in the Tablet itself. To help introduce the Tablet, Chapter One briefly surveys its historical setting. Chapter Two explores important aspects of its literary style that will be helpful to those unfamiliar with the writings of Bahá'u'lláh and the literary tradition that is their context. Chapter Three examines the different ways the Tablet has been and can be interpreted and understood. Chapter Four looks at the antecedents of the symbolism and how Bahá'u'lláh retells and re-fashions traditional stories and symbols to create his own message. This is followed by Chapter Five which contains a brief verse-by-verse analysis of the Tablet.

For those interested in further reading, there is a bibliography. This book is not an exhaustive analysis of the Tablet of the Holy Mariner, nor an attempt to create an official or authoritative interpretation of its contents. It can be expected that future authors will uncover new material that will modify, correct, or expand on much of what can be said now. Since each reader brings his or her own experience and insight to bear on the Tablet, each will no doubt find other meanings in this great work of mystical literature.

The Tablet of the Holy Mariner

Translation by Shoghi Effendi
Illustrations by Michael Sours

The Tablet of the Holy Mariner

HE IS THE GRACIOUS,
THE WELL-BELOVED!

1. O Holy Mariner!
   Bid thine ark of eternity appear
   before the Celestial Concourse,
   Glorified be my Lord, the All-Glorious!

2. Launch it upon the ancient sea, in His Name,
   the Most Wondrous,
   Glorified be my Lord, the All-Glorious!

3. And let the angelic spirits enter,
   in the Name of God, the Most High.
   Glorified be my Lord, the All-Glorious!

4. Unmoor it, then, that it may sail
   upon the ocean of glory,
   Glorified be my Lord, the All-Glorious!

5. Haply the dwellers therein may attain
   the retreats of nearness in the everlasting realm.
   Glorified be my Lord, the All-Glorious!

6. Having reached the sacred strand,
   the shore of the crimson seas,
   Glorified be my Lord, the All-Glorious!

7 Bid them issue forth
and attain this ethereal invisible station.
Glorified be my Lord, the All-Glorious!

8 A station wherein the Lord hath
in the Flame of His Beauty appeared
within the deathless tree;
Glorified be my Lord, the All-Glorious!

9 Wherein the embodiments of His Cause
cleansed themselves of self and passion;
Glorified be my Lord, the All-Glorious!

10 Around which the Glory of Moses doth
circle with the everlasting hosts;
Glorified be my Lord, the All-Glorious!

11 Wherein the Hand of God was drawn forth
from His bosom of Grandeur;
Glorified be my Lord, the All-Glorious!

12 Wherein the ark of the Cause remaineth
motionless even though to its dwellers
be declared all divine attributes.
Glorified be my Lord, the All-Glorious!

5

13. O Mariner!
    Teach them that are within the ark
    that which we have taught thee
    behind the mystic veil,
    Glorified be my Lord, the All-Glorious!

14. Perchance they may not tarry
    in the sacred snow-white spot,
    Glorified be my Lord, the All-Glorious!

15. But may soar upon the wings of the spirit
    unto that station which the Lord hath exalted
    above all mention in the worlds below,
    Glorified be my Lord, the All-Glorious!

16. May wing through space
    even as the favored birds
    in the realm of eternal reunion,
    Glorified be my Lord, the All-Glorious!

17. May know the mysteries hidden
    in the Seas of light.
    Glorified be my Lord, the All-Glorious!

18. They passed the grades of worldly limitations
    and reached that of the divine unity,
    the center of heavenly guidance.
    Glorified be my Lord, the All-Glorious!

19. They have desired to ascend unto that state
 which the Lord hath ordained
 to be above their stations.
 Glorified be my Lord, the All-Glorious!

20. Whereupon the burning meteor
 cast them out from them that abide
 in the Kingdom of His Presence,
 Glorified be my Lord, the All-Glorious!

21. And they heard the Voice of Grandeur
 raised from behind the unseen pavilion
 upon the Height of Glory:
 Glorified be my Lord, the All-Glorious!

22. "O guardian angels!
 Return them to their abode
 in the world below,
 Glorified be my Lord, the All-Glorious!

23. "Inasmuch as they have purposed to rise
 to that sphere which the wings of the celestial
 dove have never attained;
 Glorified be my Lord, the All-Glorious!

24. "Whereupon the ship of fancy standeth still
 which the minds of them that comprehend
 cannot grasp."
 Glorified be my Lord, the All-Glorious!

25 Whereupon the maid of heaven
 looked out from her exalted chamber,
 Glorified be my Lord, the All-Glorious!

26 And with her brow
 signed to the Celestial Concourse,
 Glorified be my Lord, the All-Glorious!

27 Flooding with the light of her countenance
 the heaven and the earth,
 Glorified be my Lord, the All-Glorious!

28 And as the radiance of her beauty
 shone upon the people of dust,
 Glorified be my Lord, the All-Glorious!

29 All beings were shaken in their mortal graves.
 Glorified be my Lord, the All-Glorious!

30 She then raised the call
 which no ear through all eternity
 hath ever heard,
 Glorified be my Lord, the All-Glorious!

31 And thus proclaimed: "By the Lord!
 He whose heart hath not
 the fragrance of the love
 of the exalted and glorious Arabian Youth,
 Glorified be my Lord, the All-Glorious!

32 "Can in no wise
 ascend unto the glory
 of the highest heaven."
 Glorified be my Lord, the All-Glorious!

33 Thereupon she summoned unto herself
 one maiden from her handmaidens,
 Glorified be my Lord, the All-Glorious!

34 And commanded her: "Descend into
 space from the mansions of eternity,
 Glorified be my Lord, the All-Glorious!

35 "And turn thou unto that
 which they have concealed
 in the inmost of their hearts.
 Glorified be my Lord, the All-Glorious!

36 "Shouldst thou inhale the perfume of the robe
 from the Youth that hath been hidden
 within the tabernacle of light
 by reason of that which the hands
 of the wicked have wrought,
 Glorified be my Lord, the All-Glorious!

37 "Raise a cry within thyself,
 that all the inmates of the chambers of Paradise,
 that are the embodiments of the eternal wealth,
 may understand and hearken;
 Glorified be my Lord, the All-Glorious!

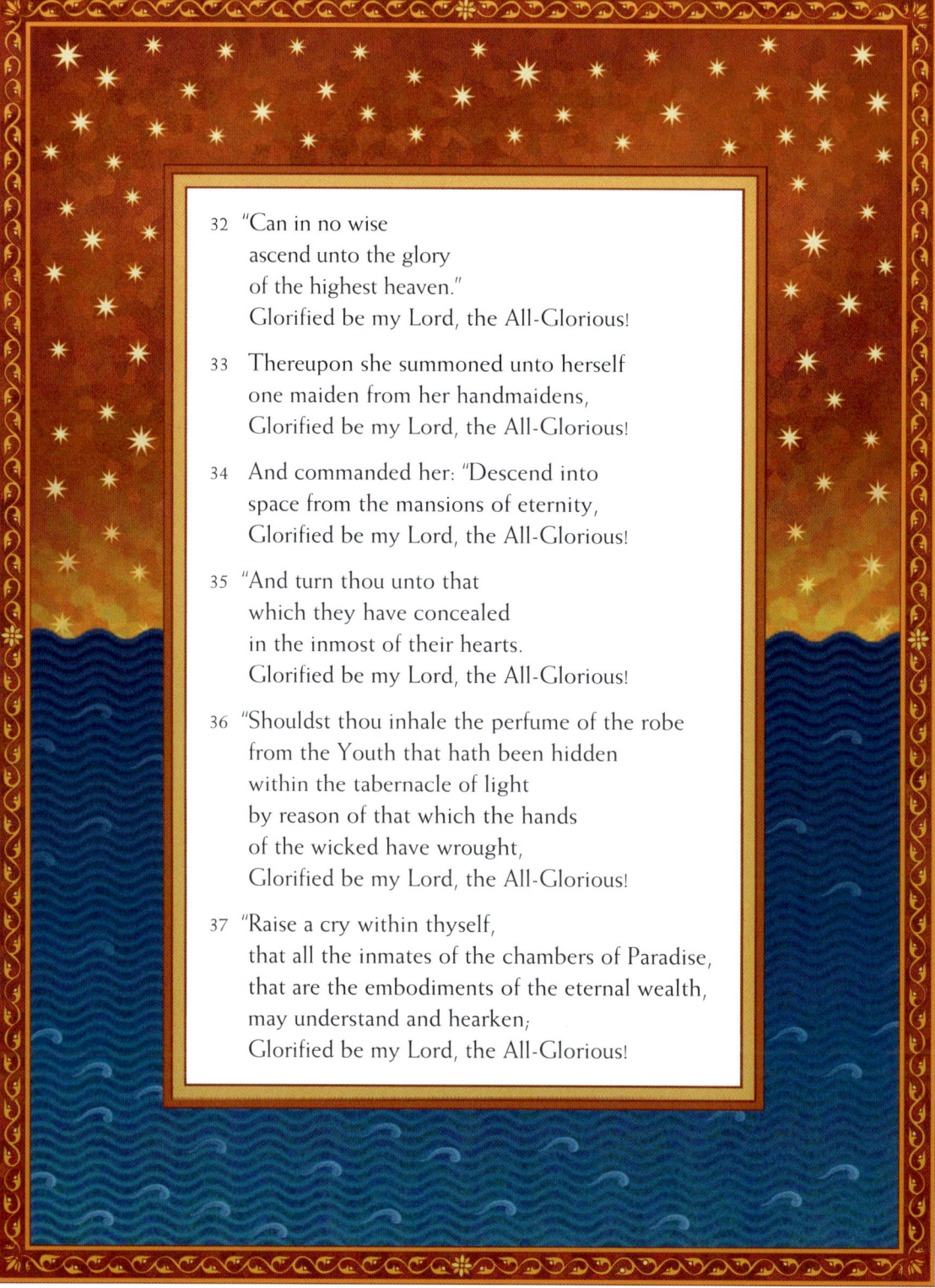

38 "That they may all come down
   from their everlasting chambers
   and tremble,
   Glorified be my Lord, the All-Glorious!

39 "And kiss their hands and feet
   for having soared to the heights of faithfulness;
   Glorified be my Lord, the All-Glorious!

40 "Perchance they may find from their robes
   the fragrance of the Beloved One."
   Glorified be my Lord, the All-Glorious!

41 Thereupon the countenance of the favored
   damsel beamed above the celestial chambers
   even as the light that shineth
   from the face of the Youth
   above His mortal temple;
   Glorified be my Lord, the All-Glorious!

42 She then descended with such an adorning
   as to illumine the heavens
   and all that is therein.
   Glorified be my Lord, the All-Glorious!

43 She bestirred herself
   and perfumed all things
   in the lands of holiness and grandeur.
   Glorified be my Lord, the All-Glorious!

44 When she reached that place
she rose to her full height
in the midmost heart of creation,
Glorified be my Lord, the All-Glorious!

45 And sought to inhale their fragrance
at a time that knoweth
neither beginning nor end.
Glorified be my Lord, the All-Glorious!

46 She found not in them
that which she did desire,
and this, verily, is but one of
His wondrous tales.
Glorified be my Lord, the All-Glorious!

47 She then cried aloud, wailed
and repaired to her own station
within her most lofty mansion,
Glorified be my Lord, the All-Glorious!

48 And then gave utterance
to one mystic word,
whispered privily by her honeyed tongue,
Glorified be my Lord, the All-Glorious!

49 And raised the call
 amidst the Celestial Concourse
 and the immortal maids of heaven:
 Glorified be my Lord, the All-Glorious!

50 "By the Lord!
 I found not from these idle claimants
 the breeze of Faithfulness!
 Glorified be my Lord, the All-Glorious!

51 "By the Lord!
 The Youth hath remained lone
 and forlorn in the land of exile
 in the hands of the ungodly."
 Glorified be my Lord, the All-Glorious!

52 She then uttered within herself
 such a cry that the Celestial Concourse
 did shriek and tremble,
 Glorified be my Lord, the All-Glorious!

53 And she fell upon the dust
 and gave up the spirit.
 It seemeth she was called
 and hearkened unto Him that summoned her
 unto the Realm on High.
 Glorified be my Lord, the All-Glorious!

The Tablet of the Holy Mariner

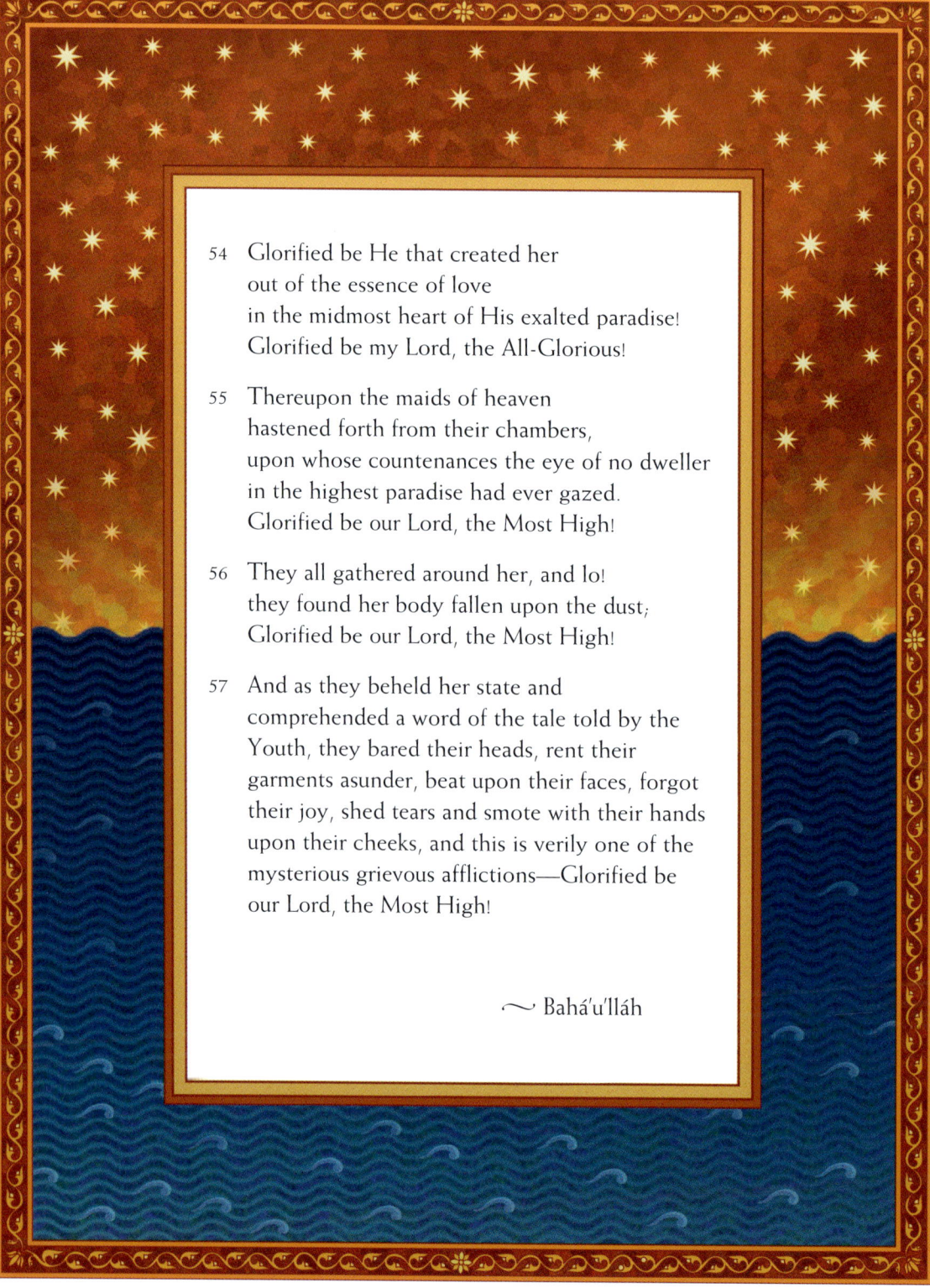

54 Glorified be He that created her
    out of the essence of love
    in the midmost heart of His exalted paradise!
    Glorified be my Lord, the All-Glorious!

55 Thereupon the maids of heaven
    hastened forth from their chambers,
    upon whose countenances the eye of no dweller
    in the highest paradise had ever gazed.
    Glorified be our Lord, the Most High!

56 They all gathered around her, and lo!
    they found her body fallen upon the dust;
    Glorified be our Lord, the Most High!

57 And as they beheld her state and comprehended a word of the tale told by the Youth, they bared their heads, rent their garments asunder, beat upon their faces, forgot their joy, shed tears and smote with their hands upon their cheeks, and this is verily one of the mysterious grievous afflictions—Glorified be our Lord, the Most High!

～ Bahá'u'lláh

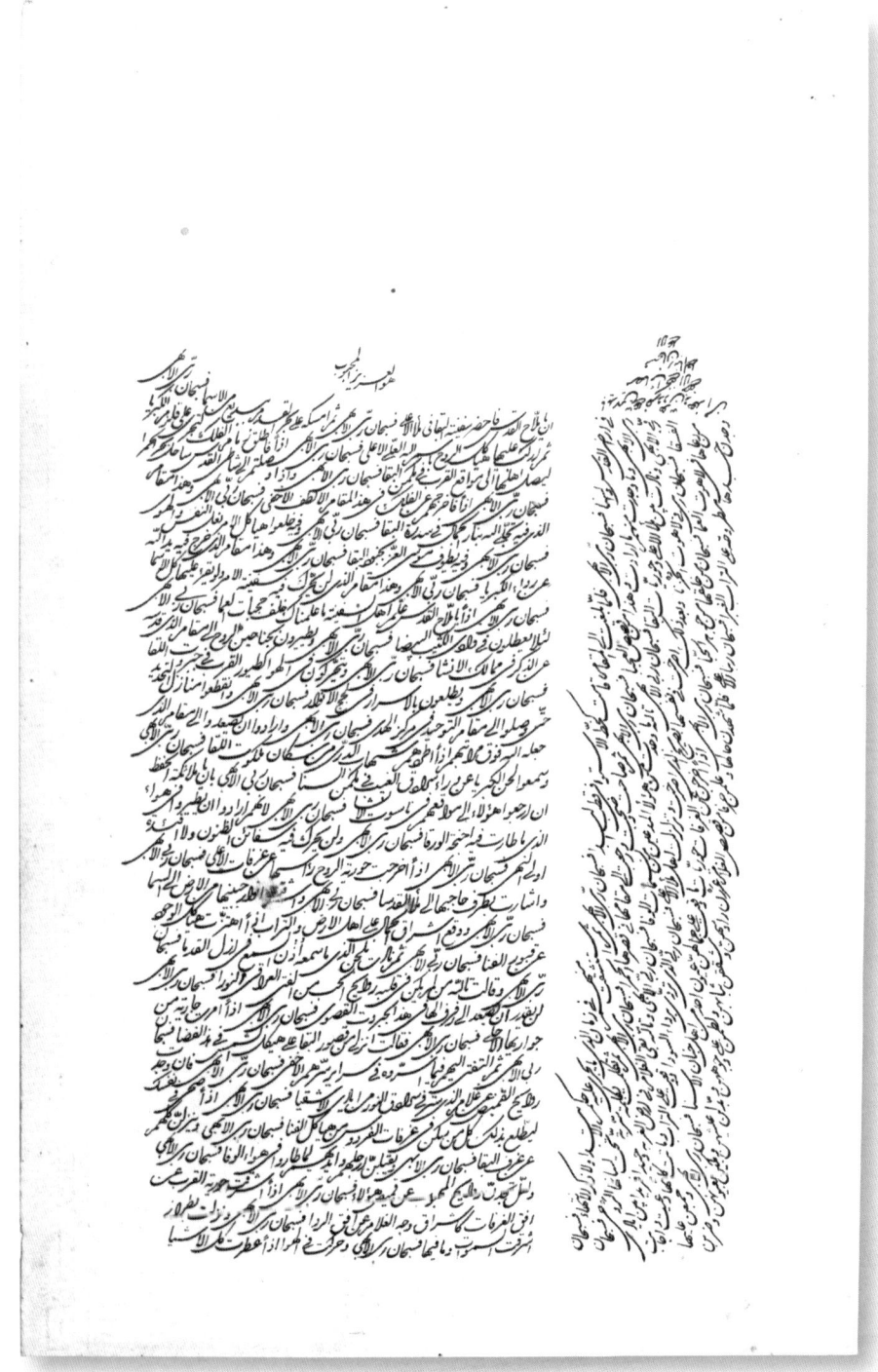

The Arabic section of the Tablet of the Holy Mariner in the hand of 'Abdu'l-Bahá, son of Bahá'u'lláh. Approximately actual size. Courtesy of the Bahá'í World Centre Archives.

1

The Authorship and Date of the Tablet

There is no barrier between the seeker and God greater than the selfish and unbefitting conduct of those who claim to be followers of God. The Tablet of the Holy Mariner was written to help seekers overcome this obstacle. It is, among other things, about search, companionship, jealousy, and betrayal—themes that have a universal or archetypal spiritual relevance to anyone seeking to live a spiritual life and draw closer to God. Nevertheless, it was originally written with reference to specific historical events foreseen by its author. Since this original context will give clarity to aspects of the Tablet's meaning, it will be beneficial to begin with a brief outline of the author's life and the circumstances surrounding the writing of the Tablet.

The author of the Tablet was Mírzá Ḥusayn 'Alí Núrí (1817–1892). He was born into the aristocracy of Persia and sometime after 1863 took the title *Bahá'u'lláh*, an Arabic phrase meaning the "Glory of God." Although his father, who was known as Mírzá Buzurg-i Núrí, held a respected position in the Persian government, Bahá'u'lláh showed no interest in politics. His humanitarianism and care for the poor won him great admiration in his home region.[1] When he was twenty-eight years old, he was sought out by a young Muslim mulla[2] who brought him a message from 'Alí-Muḥammad, a merchant from Bushihr.

'Alí-Muḥammad, who was himself only twenty-five years old, claimed to be the long-expected "Báb" (Arabic, meaning spiritual "Gate") of Muslim prophecy. In his earliest writings, he indicated that the apocalyptic Day of Judgment was approaching,[3] and acting in a role not unlike that of John the Baptist, the Báb stated that he was the herald of a new Manifestation of God.[4] These claims would soon cause unrest throughout much of Persia.[5] Bahá'u'lláh accepted these claims and lent his prestige and resources to the Báb's cause. The Báb's disciples had already set out to spread the message of the Báb throughout Persia and India[6] when Bahá'u'lláh began talking openly about the Báb's claims in his native provence of Mázindarán.[7] The rapid spread of this new spiritual movement—a movement that challenged the established orthodoxy—provoked the opposition of the civil and religious authorities. Shortly afterwards, the Báb's followers would suffer severe persecution. Many would be tortured and killed.

The Báb was first arrested in 1845, and eventually sent to a remote prison in northern Persia. In the following years most of the Báb's leading disciples would be killed by the government. In 1850, only six years after the Báb first made his claims, he was executed by a firing squad of seven hundred and fifty riflemen. This execution caused great despair among the followers of the Báb, and in 1852 several of his followers, blinded by grief and ignoring the Báb's teachings, decided to seek revenge by assassinating the shah.[8] The attempt failed, but it did provide the authorities with an added excuse to seek out the remaining followers of the Báb in order to stamp out the movement altogether.

It was during this violence that the authorities identified Bahá'u'lláh as a prominent leader of the movement and arrested him. He was imprisoned in the infamous "Síyáh-Chál" (Black Pit) of Tehran. Cleared of charges, he was released four months later and then exiled from Persia for the rest of his life. He chose the city of Baghdad, just outside the western border of Persia, as his destination and many Bábís followed. Later in life, when recounting the early experience of this imprisonment in Tehran, Bahá'u'lláh states that while he was imprisoned he decided to dedicate himself to rehabilitating the Bábí community.[9]

The Báb had taught his followers to expect the imminent appearance of "Him Whom God will make manifest," the "long-expected Remnant of God," and during the 1850s many individuals claimed to be this promised one, the anticipated spiritual leader.[10] Rather than become a source of contention among these vying claimants or those who were envious of the veneration Bahá'u'lláh received, Bahá'u'lláh chose to leave the Bábí community. Taking up the name Muḥammad-i Írání and wearing the clothes of a dervish, he left Baghdad to retire in the mountains of Iraqi Kurdistan. There he spent his time in solitude and, according to his own words, he *"contemplated no return."*[11] He was, however, discovered by the Sufis in that region and invited to the *khánaqah* (seminary) in the Kurdish town of

Authorship and Date

Sulaymaniyih.[12] When accounts of Muhammad-i Írání's holiness and wisdom reached the Bábí community in Baghdad, his identity was suspected. Two years after Bahá'u'lláh's departure from Baghdad, a messenger was sent to seek him out and to persuade him to return.

The situation among the Bábís had become grave; the believers were in a state of moral disintegration. The community was, in fact, edging toward extinction. Those who had assumed the leadership of the community had failed to offer any real guidance. Many of the remaining Bábís were demoralized and confused, and they naturally welcomed the return of Bahá'u'lláh. His own references to this period suggest that he would have given up on the Bábí community and remained a dervish for the rest of his life had it not been for the grief he felt at the thought that all the blood shed in the path of the Báb would have been shed in vain. Bahá'u'lláh had himself been close to many of the Bábís who had been killed, some of them in their youth. That tragic period, when so many people died, would color his writings for the remaining years of his life.

After his return to Baghdad in 1856 things began to improve. Bahá'u'lláh wrote several of his most important works—the The Seven Valleys,[13] the Kitáb-i Íqán (Book of Certitude), and the Hidden Book of Fátimih, later known as The Hidden Words. These works provided much needed spiritual guidance, doctrinal clarity, and ethical inspiration to the Bábí community. The Book of Certitude was important, especially for clarifying many of the Báb's religious claims and theological writings.

In March 1863, seven years after his return from the mountains of Sulaymaniyih, Bahá'u'lláh gathered together with some of his companions in a countryside garden near Baghdad to celebrate the Persian New Year (March 21). It was on the fifth day (March 26) of this celebration that the Tablet of the Holy Mariner (Arabic: Lawh-i Malláhu'l-Quds) was written and then read aloud by Bahá'u'lláh's amanuensis, Mírzá Áqá Ján. These events were later recorded in a historical account written by Nabíl-i A'zam, one of Bahá'u'lláh's followers.[14] When this history was written, sometime in the 1880s, many of those present in the garden, including Bahá'u'lláh and Mírzá Áqá Ján, were still alive. Although there is surprisingly little available information about this occasion, there is no reason to doubt the traditional account of either the authorship or date of the Tablet.[15]

At the time Bahá'u'lláh wrote the Tablet of the Holy Mariner he was forty-six years old. In the following month of April, Bahá'u'lláh announced that he was the one the Báb had referred to as "Him Whom God shall make manifest." This claim, in whatever way it was indicated, was within a short period acknowledged readily by nearly all Bábís.[16] Sometime after 1866, the Bábís came to be known as "Bahá'ís," followers of Bahá'u'lláh.

Some Bábís, however, resented deeply the devotion Bahá'u'lláh received and, wishing presumably to draw attention to themselves and retain their earlier prominence in the community, sought to oppose and even murder him. In the years to come, most of Bahá'u'lláh's greatest trials, like his earlier imprisonment in the Síyáh-Chál, would be brought on by those who professed allegiance to the Báb, but who in actual fact had betrayed his teachings. The Tablet of the Holy Mariner anticipates the opposition Bahá'u'lláh would encounter.

The main opponents of Bahá'u'lláh were his own half-brother Mírzá Yahyá and Sayyid Muhammad-i Isfahání, both of whom appear to have been motivated by jealousy and a hunger for leadership. These historical details—and in particular, Mírzá Yahyá's failed attempt to assert himself as the leader of the Bábí community—provide the context of the Tablet of the Holy Mariner and suggest why the Tablet has been interpreted primarily from the point of view of internal strife within the community of believers. However, the archetypal nature of its symbolism enables the Tablet to be viewed in a broader spiritual context. Many passages of the Tablet also deal with various aspects of spiritual development. At one time or another, most every spiritual seeker has to confront the issues raised by this Tablet, whether from within or without.

2

The Literary Style of the Tablet

The Tablet of the Holy Mariner (*Lawḥ-i Mallāḥu'l-Quds*) exists in two versions, one written in Arabic and the other in Persian, together comprising about ten to fifteen pages of text. The Arabic and Persian versions can be read as separate works as each stands easily on its own. The Persian prose text contains the same allegory (of the Mariner and Ark) as the first portion of the Arabic text, but the Persian Tablet uses different symbolism more characteristic of Persian mystical literature and contains more explicit exhortations.[1] Both the Persian and the Arabic present a beautiful and compelling use of allegory, but the allegory in the Arabic text is more detailed and occupies the full content of the Tablet. The Arabic version is also very different in style from the Persian, being more opaque and rhythmic.

The Arabic version was translated into English by Shoghi Effendi and first published in the May 1922 edition of the early Bahá'í periodical *Star of the West*. At that time, it was printed with the title a "Song of the Holy Mariner." Since each verse is followed by a refrain with the words "Glorified be my Lord, the All-Glorious!", with the exception of the last three verses that are followed by the refrain "Glorified be our Lord, the Most High!", the refrains were regarded as a chorus to the main verses, and this is probably why it was designated as a song.[2] This early translation by Shoghi Effendi is the one still in print today, and it is the translation used in this commentary.[3] Counting the opening invocation, the translation of the Arabic text contains 115 verses including the refrains.

The Arabic portion of the Tablet of the Holy Mariner is an allegory from beginning to end. It is written in the form of a soliloquy which, for the sake of analysis, can be divided into two main scenes, or acts, forming one dramatic narration. Bahá'u'lláh is the narrator (v. 46, 57) or storyteller who in the first act is speaking to himself, the Mariner. To summarize the outward form of the allegory briefly: In act one, the Mariner is called upon to launch a ship designated the *"ark of eternity,"* and the faithful are invited to board it. The ship is unmoored and put out to sea on a journey to the tree of life situated beyond the shore of the crimson seas. There the Mariner teaches the passengers the mysteries of God which enable them to ascend like angels through the realms of heaven. Some of these passengers desire a station for themselves that is beyond their nature to achieve. Consequently, they are cast out of heaven by a meteor and returned to earth by the guardian angels.

In act two, the Maid of Heaven—a feminine personification of the spirit of God and continuation of the angelic concourse described in the preceding verses—appears and announces that the highest heaven is inaccessible to those who do not possess the love of God. The Maid of Heaven calls upon one of her handmaidens. She instructs her to seek out those who are faithful to God so that the dwellers of the celestial realm may pay homage to them. The handmaiden descends to earth and conducts her search, but finds no one. She then returns to heaven and proclaims the state of treachery that exists on earth. Stricken by grief over humanity's unfaithfulness, the handmaiden falls down and dies. Her spirit returns to God, and the other maidens of the celestial concourse gather around her body grieving. Like a theatrical drama, this tragic scene of the dying handmaiden closes the performance and ends the poem.

Despite this tragic ending, there are good reasons *not* to read the message of the Tablet pessimistically. Once viewed in its cultural setting and in the broader context of Bahá'u'lláh's own writings about spirituality, it becomes clear that the message of the Tablet is essentially positive. This will be explained further in the commentary in Chapter 5.

With regard to the dramatic characteristics and tragic imagery of the Tablet, it is worth pointing out that in Bahá'u'lláh's homeland there were a number of cultural currents that Bahá'u'lláh may have drawn upon to create the Tablet's form and symbolic content. One may have been the growing interest in theatrical performances in Persia, and the other, devotional practices such as those practiced by the Sufi orders.

With regard to theatre, such performances were called *ta'ziyah*[4] and focused originally on the reenactment of a series of tragic tales all connected in some way

Etching from S. G. W. Benjamin's *Persia and the Persians* (1886) labeled "The Takiêh, or Royal Theatre."

to the martyrdom of the Imám Ḥusayn.[5] In the nineteenth century, the art form was perhaps in its golden age. As a religious and public service, the Persian aristocracy—the class to which Bahá'u'lláh belonged—provided the funds necessary for theatres, known as *takiyeh*, to be built in the cities and towns. Ta'ziyah incorporated narration, dramatic performance, song or chanting, and a high degree of audience participation. This was a well-known, widely performed annual event that reached all levels of society. Its content was essentially spiritual in focus, rather than historical, and it was accepted that participation had a redemptive value for the audience. There are certain characteristics in the Tablet of the Holy Mariner that suggest affinity with this cultural phenomena.

Anyone reading the Tablet of the Holy Mariner, with its refrains, will easily perceive that this Tablet was intended to be read aloud. Such recitation was in fact the way the Tablet was first introduced. If recited effectively, the Tablet has an extraordinary aesthetic quality that is profoundly moving. Like ta'ziyah, this aesthetic effect can be enhanced further by the use of various reciters working together and the structure of the Tablet lends itself to such an arrangement. For example, the Tablet contains three monologues by three different persona: the Voice of Grandeur (v. 21), the Maid of Heaven (v. 31–40), and the Maiden's handmaiden (v. 50–51). Since the refrains interrupt these monologues, clarity is heightened naturally by using two distinct readers to separate the main narration and monologues from the refrains. The refrains can be taken up easily by an arranged chorus or even the audience. Further dramatic effect could be added by using different reciters for each of the monologues. Whatever the approach, the Tablet lends itself naturally to dramatic recitation. While there is no concrete evidence to indicate that Bahá'u'lláh intended that the Tablet should be the text, or basis for a script, for religious theatre, all these above features do find parallels in the popular ta'ziyah of Bahá'u'lláh's day.

In addition to its form, there are many elements in the actual content and symbolism of the Tablet that correspond to the ta'ziyah, passion play for Imám Ḥusayn. There is, for example, in the latter a central Maid of Heaven who calls on her handmaiden, who swoons, and whose grief-stricken body is then surrounded by other maids of heaven. Unlike Bahá'u'lláh's soliloquy, the Maid of Heaven in the ta'ziyah is identified as Fáṭimih, the daughter of Muḥammad, and it is she who swoons from grief, not her handmaiden. The maids of heaven also comes forth to gather around the grief-stricken Fáṭimih. But in the passion play, Gabriel explains to Fáṭimih that the maidens are the brides of the companions of the Prophet Muḥammad, whereas in Bahá'u'lláh's soliloquy the maidens are ones who have never been seen before. The passion play narrative also continues after this scene, whereas Bahá'u'lláh's narrative ends abruptly without further elaboration. Whatever the differences, the similarities show that the basic symbolism in Bahá'u'lláh's Tablet is rooted firmly in the popular culture of his time. Bahá'u'lláh has lifted the symbolism out of its Islamic context, and moved it to a Bábí mystical context. Originality is not found in the particular symbols used, but rather in their subtle reshaping.[6]

In addition to ta'ziyah, the Tablet reflects features of Sufi devotional practice. The repeating refrains are not always printed in the text of published translations, but there are good reasons to regard this structure as important. In mystical religious societies, such as the Sufi orders, the use of chanting and rhythmic recitations are common. It is probable that Bahá'u'lláh was acquainted with such activities and may have participated in them while in Sulaymaniyih. Even before he went to Sulaymáníyyih, Nabíl records that when Bahá'u'lláh was imprisoned with other Bábís in 1852, he taught them to chant rhythmically certain verses. One row of Bábís would recite: *"God is sufficient unto me; He verily is the*

All-sufficing!"; while the other row would reply: *"In Him let the trusting trust."*[7] The importance of beautiful recitation can be seen in Bahá'u'lláh's own statements: *"Those who recite the verses of the All-Merciful in the most melodious of tones will perceive in them that which the sovereignty of earth and heaven can never be compared,"* and *"Whoever hath been transported by the rapture born of adoration for My Name, the Most Compassionate, will recite the verses of God in such wise as to captivate the hearts of those yet wrapped in slumber."*[8]

The artistic construction of the Tablet of the Holy Mariner indicates that it is meant to be experienced, not just studied like a commentary or read simply for instruction. While the message of the text helps focus the mind on the path to God, the aesthetic dimension of the Tablet, especially the dramatic rhythmic character of the refrains, helps heighten the emotional bond to that path. In Evelyn Underhill's book, *Mysticism*, a pioneering study of the nature and development of spiritual consciousness, she makes this interesting comment about rhythmic language and mysticism:

> The mystic, as a rule, cannot wholly do without symbol and image, inadequate to his vision though they must always be: for his experience must be expressed if it is to be communicated, and its actuality is inexpressible except in some side-long way, some hint or parallel which will stimulate the dormant intuition of the reader, and convey, as all poetic language does, something beyond its surface sense. Hence the large part which is played in all mystical writings by symbolism and imagery; and also by that rhythmic and exalted language which induces in sensitive persons something of the languid ecstasy of dream. The close connection between rhythm and heightened states of consciousness is as yet little understood.[9]

The use of rhythm can take many forms, such as the chanting of sacred words or the back-and-forth of a dialogue in a mystical treatise. It is common among Sufis to engage in the practice of reciting the Greatest Name (Alláh) continuously with the aim of making the remembrance of God a part of their subconscious as well as their conscious experience.[10] Bahá'u'lláh also encouraged the practice of saying a variation of the Greatest Name (Alláh-u Abhá, lit. God is Glorious) ninety-five times every day.[11]

In addition to the Tablet of the Holy Mariner, Bahá'u'lláh uses various forms of repetition in other Tablets to create a strong sense of rhythm. The Fire Tablet and the Long Healing Prayer are two such examples.[12] Another example is a text Bahá'u'lláh incorporated into other Tablets, sometimes referred to by Bahá'ís as "These Perspicuous Verses." It uses a series of questions answered with rhetorical exclamations. These popular devotional texts are some of Bahá'u'lláh's most dramatic and moving works.[13]

With regard to the Tablet of the Holy Mariner, Bahá'u'lláh uses different forms of repetition to build the overall rhythmic style. In addition to the repeating refrains, there is the use of repeating words and invocations at the beginning of sentences. There is also a less certain use of synonyms and restatement of the same thought. In some passages, for example, Bahá'u'lláh builds on a theme of the sailing ark or the ascent to heaven through a series of statements with similar meanings. The extent to which he is restating the same theme in different words or developing it in stages is elusive. Each idea is close enough in meaning to create an indefinite distinction. Is the *"ancient sea"* (v. 2) different from the *"ocean of glory"* (v. 4), or the same reality described twice? Or can it be both? Whichever way it is understood, the end effect of this characteristic is to add to the Tablet's sense of rhythm.

Most importantly, the Tablet's form cannot be separated from its message. It is essential that the person participating in the Tablet be receptive to its message. In Nabíl's narrative, he mentions frequently the dreams and visions of devoted seekers. If the mind is first oriented to the divine and spiritual realities, then when it is in a state most removed from the mundane concerns of this world, such as deep meditation or sleep, it is susceptible to experiences which can be interpreted in illuminating ways. The use of rhythm helps lift the receptive mind above temporal concerns and allows the heart to grasp the message more deeply.

3

The Interpretation of the Tablet

Before discussing actual interpretations of the Tablet, it will be helpful to first consider the act of interpretation, what it means, and the necessary qualifications of the seeker who wishes to recite the Tablet and to understand its deeper message.

With regard to what it means to interpret, discussions in the Islamic world are influenced by distinct traditions. Most significantly, there is a stream of thought that sees interpretation (*tafsír*) as harmful and in error. Since Western thinking tends to preclude the idea that perception can take place without some personal interpretation, it is helpful to consider what is meant by "interpretation" in the Islamic context. The Islamic outlook is based on acceptance of certain traditional sayings such as, "the person who makes interpretations or commentary according to his own opinion makes himself an unbeliever."[1] This tradition has been understood and applied in various ways depending upon such matters as the type of verses being discussed, whether the interpretation pertains to the outward or inner sense of the scriptural verses, and depending upon who is believed to have the authority to interpret. Among Shí'í Muslims, the ability to interpret the inner sense (*ta'wíl*) is restricted to the Imáms. Shí'í commentators generally escape the accusation of interpretation by purporting to adhere to a literal interpretation or by elucidating the text via reference to other quranic passages or the sayings of the Imáms.

This approach presents a somewhat novel idea to Western thought, that is, literal interpretation is not counted as interpretation. To be fair, the use of the word "literal" is somewhat misleading, as it refers simply to the outward or evident meaning. In Bahá'u'lláh's writings, this idea is expressed with regard to commandments and laws which he says must be understood according to their evident meaning.[2] However, Bahá'u'lláh does not apply this idea to all types of sacred literature, nor does he affirm the belief that the understanding of the inner significance of scripture is only accessible to the seeker with the aid of an Imám.

In Bahá'u'lláh's version of the Seven Valleys, for example, Bahá'u'lláh praises Shaykh Muhyi'd-Dín for his interpretation of the common sparrow, the Persian term for which is *gunjishk*. Bahá'u'lláh then adds his own alternative interpretation that uses a seemingly arbitrary approach that extracts meaning from each of the letters in the word gunjishk.[3] He writes, that *"on every plane, to every letter a meaning is allotted which relateth to that plane. Indeed, the wayfarer findeth a secret in every name, a mystery in every letter."*[4] In this example, Bahá'u'lláh freely interprets the humble gunjishk as representing holiness, and each letter is commented on accordingly to reinforce this idea. In many ways, this approach, especially the commentary on each letter, represents an esoteric type of interpretation.

This encouragement for personal interpretation is not limited to works of mystical poetry. In the Book of Certitude, written only a few years later, Bahá'u'lláh speaks at length about the interpretation of scripture, giving examples for the explicit purpose of enabling seekers to understand other verses not specifically explained.[5] He also criticizes religious leaders who have failed to understand the symbolic nature of most sacred scripture, especially the prophetic verses, indicating clearly that it is an error to insist on literal interpretations of such verses.[6] He argues that by insisting on literal interpretations, religious leaders often cause people to be misled about the true intention of the sacred books. All these statements indicate that personal interpretation of scripture according to methods that recognize the symbolism in the texts, is fundamental to an illumined understanding of the sacred books. Bahá'u'lláh both encourages personal interpretation as a necessary aspect of the seeker's search for truth and tries to liberate seekers from the oppression of those who try to suppress individual interpretation by insisting on literalism, an approach often based on a misuse of traditional sayings about the evils of interpretation.

From the context of these instances, some significant points emerge with regard to the meaning of interpretation and the best approach to use: First, although all verses may have a inner significance, the evident or outward meaning of the *commandments* must not be ignored,[7] and this is the primary significance of what it means to forbid interpretation. Second, elucidating the meaning of texts via the inspired sayings and explanations of the appointed spiritual guides[8] is acceptable and is also not considered as "interpretation" in the negative sense. Third, this type of interpretation, which might be better called *elucidation*, is when the commentator uncovers meanings based on some existing scriptural evidence rather than mere personal opinion. In fact, this is the kind of interpretation that is acceptable and encouraged; although, it should be understood that such personal applications may not necessarily be correct.[9] Methodologically, most commentaries, whether Muslim, Christian, Buddhist, Bahá'í, or otherwise, fall into this category, since most commentators base their ideas about one set of verses by reference to other verses. Unlike mere unsupported personal opinion, this method has the benefit of establishing a contextual boundary that helps limit unwarranted conjecture, even if the conclusions are in error.[10]

Bahá'u'lláh's teachings also reflect significant parallels with Sufi ideas about interpretation. Based on the quranic verse *"Question the people of the Remembrance, if it should be that you do not know,"*[11] many Sufis understand that the discipline of remembering God is the key that unveils the inner meaning of the verses. Through prayer and chanting the name of God, Sufi orders seek to be the people of the remembrance of God. This *remembrance* (*al-dhikr*) is, however, understood by the Shí'ís as referring to the Imáms. In Bábí scripture the Báb identifies the prophets and himself as the Remembrance of God, making his followers the people of the Remembrance.[12] These Bábí teachings do not, however, contradict or negate the Sufi point of view. The Prophets are the Remembrance of God *par excellence*, whereas all seekers in their own degree should seek to attain the station of being the people of the Remembrance of God.

This basic discipline of directing one's thoughts toward God, and away from attachments to this world by remembering God, is essential to all who seek to understand the divine mysteries. In Bahá'u'lláh's writings the condition of the seeker is linked with the seeker's ability to unveil the meaning of the scriptures and understand the divine teachings.[13] Bahá'u'lláh, for example, stresses detachment from preconceived ideas, acquired learning, material concerns, as well as love and hate, as a prerequisite to illumination.[14] With these thoughts in mind, the seeker reading the Tablet of the Holy Mariner will not want to merely pick up the text and read it as if it were any kind of literature. A determined seeker will want to give consideration to situating one's self in a reverent manner, freeing one's thoughts of material concerns and centering one's attention on God. Rather than just reading the text, the seeker participates with the text in a quest for illumination. That is, the process is twofold. The reader prepares his or her heart through detachment and sanctification, and in this way attains a condition of spiritual receptiveness while the text imparts meaning.

With regard to the Tablet of the Holy Mariner, it is axiomatic that the meaning of such allegorical language cannot be discovered by reading the text in its literal sense. It is also clear that this type of literature is capable of revealing many meanings applicable to various situations, each valid in its own way. For the purposes of this introductory study, there are two basic perspectives from which the Tablet will be approached: One is to relate the message of the Tablet solely to historical events within the Bahá'í community. In the same way, for example, the Christian Book of Revelation might be understood from a purely Christian-centric and historical perspective. The other way of understanding the Tablet involves seeing it as a broader, more universal, more personal message applicable to anyone seeking after spiritual truth, regardless of religious identity or association. Whichever way the Tablet is understood, the reader who is able to relate the spiritual import of each verse to his or her own self will be approaching the text in a most beneficial light.

Using this first approach—which, for convenience, can be called the "historical" approach—the Tablet is seen primarily in its original historical setting. In this sense, the Tablet is a prediction of the opposition Bahá'u'lláh faced as the spiritual leader of a religious community which after 1863, was composed of both former Bábís and new converts. From this perspective, the reading of the Tablet in the garden of Baghdad among a gathering of friends and companions on the eve of Bahá'u'lláh's departure for Istanbul suggests parallels to the account of Jesus in the garden of Gethsemane prophesying his followers' betrayal of him.[15]

The ark of eternity represents the teachings that preserve the unity and well being of the community of God.[16] The rebellion and expulsion of the angels from heaven represents expulsion from the community of those who seek to create schism, that is, those who seek to establish a Bábí community that follows a leadership separate from and opposed to that of Bahá'u'lláh. The rebellious angels are none other than Bahá'u'lláh's half-brother, Mírzá Yahyá, and Sayyid Muhammad-i Isfahání who sought to murder Bahá'u'lláh in an ongoing, but failed, attempt to make themselves the leaders of the Bábí community.[17]

The quest of the handmaiden can likewise be understood as a quest to discover the truth of those claimants who opposed Bahá'u'lláh. From this point of view, the Tablet is most relevant to historical events occurring between 1863, and no later than 1892, when Bahá'u'lláh passed away and leadership of the community passed to his son, 'Abdu'l-Bahá. From the point of view of the historical development of the Bahá'í community and its unity, this prediction of betrayal, coupled with its assurance of victory over the schismatics (as indicated in the expulsion of the rebellious angels), is the most important and central element in the Tablet.

This same predictive and historical interpretation can also have an archetypal dimension. That is, the Tablet can be understood as foreshadowing any struggle over leadership in the community initiated by persons who have no rightful claim to that position. This type of interpretation was made by 'Abdu'l-Bahá in 1921, during the days of Riḍván, an annual festival commemorating the original Riḍván festival of 1863, which took place shortly after Bahá'u'lláh first made his claims known.[18] On that anniversary celebration, 'Abdu'l-Bahá called attention to the Tablet of the Holy Mariner in a letter to the Bahá'í community.[19] He pointed out that the community was strong and prospering, but that there were some who sought to stir up trouble. In this letter he wrote, *"exercise the utmost care and day and night be on your guard that thereby the tyrant may not inflict an injury. Study the Tablet of the Holy Mariner that ye may know the truth and consider that the Blessed Beauty* [Bahá'u'lláh][20] *hath fully foretold future events."* The warning in this letter is understood widely among Bahá'ís as an anticipation of how some from among the believers would betray 'Abdu'l-Bahá by turning against his appointed successor, Shoghi Effendi—which in fact did happen.[21]

In this sense, the ark of eternity represents the covenant community as defined in 'Abdu'l-Bahá's last Will and Testament, a document that appoints authoritatively Shoghi Effendi as the guardian of the Bahá'í community. Through recognition of this appointment, the community would be preserved from schism and saved from the despair caused by all those who would be tempted to rush forward claiming leadership. In one sense, the Tablet foresaw originally that Bahá'u'lláh would be betrayed by his half-brother Mírzá Yaḥyá. But 'Abdu'l-Bahá also saw the Tablet as having a broader archetypal message applicable to similar later events. In fact, from a spiritual point of view the Tablet continues to have this historical significance to Bahá'ís as they work to preserve the unity of the Bahá'í community. The ability of Bahá'u'lláh's covenant to preserve the community from division is viewed by Bahá'ís as a unique feature of central importance, distinguishing Bahá'ís from past religious communities.

Beyond this type of historical interpretation, it is apparent that the Tablet has many other dimensions. It is obvious that the themes of jealousy, ambition, and betrayal are not unique to Bahá'í history. People in any religious community, as well as seekers who make no explicit identifications with organized religion are likely to encounter these human tendencies. In fact, there is no greater obstacle for seekers than the conduct of people who claim to be followers of God. If anyone were to ask a person who had given up religion, what was the reason for his or her disillusionment, many would no doubt respond with stories of betrayal, worldly ambition, and jealousy. Sincere faith is often extinguished by the pain and shock of the hypocrisy and faithlessness of others. The Tablet of the Holy Mariner is an important warning to such seekers. It seeks to alert and prepare them at the start of their journey, so that they may be preserved from such tests or resurrected back into the life of faith should they become disillusioned. It is through coming together that people can combine their collective energies for the benefit of others, but this energy also is a power that can be exploited for selfish gain. Wherever there is power, prestige, or influence, there will be opportunities for ambition, pride, and corruption. As Jesus warned his followers in his last sermon: *"Wherever the corpse is, there the vultures will gather."*[22] Those seeking the things of this world masquerade as angels of light and the faith of innocent seekers is injured by them. Bahá'u'lláh knew and foresaw these things. In the Tablet of the Holy Mariner he reveals a vision of how such inevitable tragedies can be a door to greater enlightenment. The seeker sets out absorbed in anticipation of the ecstasy of the beatific vision, unaware that the path of faith is not without pain and struggle. This Tablet reorients the seeker's expectations, explaining that the unveiled bride of heaven must be sought out even in the pain of the spiritual path.

The Tablet is not, however, just about betrayal. Another dominant feature is the theme of how to draw near to God and attain the divine presence. The themes of betrayal and faithlessness are present in much of the Tablet, but so is the positive counterpart of mystic disclosure, the instruction of how to ascend to the higher worlds of God, and the promise of attaining the divine presence. These themes of divine disclosure and divine meeting can be approached from both a Bahá'í or from a broader religious perspective.

It is also possible to read the Tablet from a personal point of view—identifying our own spiritual natures with the forces of light and darkness described in the Tablet. The ark of eternity, the fallen angels, the land of exile, the Mariner, the Arabian Youth, or the celestial maidens described in the Tablet can all be understood as personal and interior. From this perspective, the reader is not a passive observer, but rather an active participant. In Bahá'u'lláh's writings, the unity of God, unity of religion, and unity of humankind are the greatest and most central spiritual truths. In its broadest sense, entering the ark of eternity is the realization of this unity, which has its origin in the oneness of God. And, this oneness of God is the foundation of the oneness of humanity and the oneness of all religious traditions. Division arises from human perceptions and limitations. Through this realization, the dweller in the ark can sail safely over all the religious seas. Religious strife, whether originating in envy, ambition, or ignorance, leads to expulsion from heaven. Likewise, every seeker's attachments and prejudices have caused the Beloved to be exiled to a distant land. The fragrance of the love of the Beloved is the only dowry the inhabitants of the celestial realm will accept. The seeker's love is not true unless it recognizes the Beloved, no matter what garment the Beloved chooses to wear, whether it be the garment of Christianity, Islam, Hinduism, or some other religious system.

The concept of discovering the divine reality within our own selves is basic to mystical writing. Bahá'u'lláh writes, that the seeker *"rideth in the ark of 'We shall show them our signs in the regions and in themselves.'"*[23] In his book, the Hidden Words, Bahá'u'lláh addresses this theme in many passages. He for example tells the seeker, "My [God's] *love is in thee, know it, that thou mayest find Me near unto thee,"* *"Thou art My lamp and My light is in thee,"* *"turn thy sight unto thyself, that thou mayest find Me standing within thee, mighty, powerful and self-subsisting,"* *"thy hearing is My hearing,"* *"thy sight is My sight,"* and so on.[24]

Or in the words of the Rúmí:

> This mention of Moses has become a shackle on men's minds—they think these stories happened long ago. The mention of Moses serves as a mask: Moses' light is your own coin, oh good man! Moses and Pharoah are in your own existence—you must seek these two adversaries in yourself.[25]

It is worth noting that, in Bahá'u'lláh's writings, finding God within is not the same as becoming God incarnate, or God in totality, or assuming that the collective totality of creation is God. He writes, *"minds cannot grasp Me nor hearts contain Me."*[26] In addition to the question of how the Tablet can be understood, it is worth going beyond the basic allegory and asking what the Tablet tells us about Bahá'u'lláh's religious views. There are no direct statements in the Tablet from which Bahá'u'lláh's own theological views and doctrinal beliefs can be constructed without elucidation by way of other texts. Nevertheless, some verses, such as the reference to *"that sphere which the wings of the celestial dove have never attained"* or the Maiden's proclamation, *"He whose heart hath not the fragrance of the love of the exalted and glorious Arabian Youth can in no wise ascend unto the glory of the highest heaven"* suggest a familiar dualistic and redemptive theism well known to Judaism, Christianity, and Islam.

Despite the lack of clear doctrinal statements in the Tablet, it is possible to infer many things from the symbolism itself. Evelyn Underhill suggested that there were three basic groups of mystical symbols, each determined by a certain view of God.[27] Those who conceive of God as remote and transcendent employ the symbolism of arduous journeys, such as John Bunyan's *Pilgrim's Progress* or Farídu'd-Dín 'Attár's seven valleys in *The Conference of the Birds*. Those who conceive of God as an intimate and personal relation employ the symbolism of earthly passion, such as courtship and marriage symbolism. Those who conceive of God as a transcendent Reality immanent in this world and in the self, Whose presence is to be attained through self improvement, use the symbolism of alchemy and the hidden treasure. Throughout history people have chosen to emphasize certain methodologies in favor of others, such as gnosis, devotion, or a renunciatory life. But it is clear that these methodologies usually overlap to some degree, as do the different forms of symbolisms.

Certainly, in Bahá'u'lláh's writings all three of these forms can be observed. Bahá'u'lláh's Seven Valleys follows, in construction, the journey symbolism. His early Tablet, the Ode of the Dove, employs the earthly passion symbolism. Scattered references to alchemy and the hidden treasure can also be observed in Bahá'u'lláh's writings.[28] But in the Tablet of the Holy Mariner traces of all three are evident. The sailing of the ark, the ascent to heaven, as well as the handmaiden's search, are all variations on the journey symbolism. The use of the maidens and the Beloved are derived from the the earthly passion symbolism. The Youth who is hidden in the land of exile suggests the hidden treasure symbolism. Together, these symbols suggest a religious perspective wherein God is both immanent and transcendent, approached through knowledge, through devotion, and through spiritual self-improvement.

With regard to religious anthropology, the Tablet's symbolism suggests that human beings have a spiritual destiny, that this destiny is attained through the direct intervention of God, unfolds in stages, and is determined by free will. With regard to theology, God is personal and immanent while being transcendent and beyond human grasp. While a seeker can ascend spiritually, God is ultimately beyond human attainment or comprehension. With regard to soteriology, the path to God is one of purification and devotion. The Tablet's core ethical and spiritual teaching is expressed in its message about detachment, purity, humility, servitude, self-sacrifice, truthfulness, faithfulness, and love. The Tablet warns of the errors of

Interpretation

pride, vanity, idleness, infidelity, and deception. God's part in human redemption is evident in the presence of the Mariner, the Guide, who directs the way to the spiritual life, providing the Ark and leading its passengers to the eternal Tree and ascent to heaven.

The Tablet also presents a hierarchal world view—both in terms of stages or levels, as well as with regard to the Maid of Heaven and her handmaidens. Some religious scholars consider this type of cosmological symbolism to be evidence of an oppressive patriarchalism.[29] But it is worth noting that the portrait of the maidens here is one of empowerment. The Maid of Heaven's radiance is capable of shaking all beings in their mortal graves (v. 29). She holds the commanding role in the latter portion of the Tablet, and when she calls out for assistance, it is to a handmaiden, another feminine personification of the divine. The feminine gender is not only employed symbolically to signify spiritual wisdom (light) in its highest form, but is also represented in an active, not passive, way. It is celestial women who act as the chief agents of God in this symbolic divine cosmology and who occupy the center stage for much of the allegory.

4

THE SYMBOLISM OF THE TABLET

Bahá'u'lláh's writings are full of symbolism, mostly in the form of metaphors and similes based on well-known religious themes, places, and personages. This is especially so with the Tablet of the Holy Mariner which is an allegory from start to finish. Since such imagery was common to the literature and oral tradition of Persia, most of his companions would have appreciated the main significance of what he had written. Bahá'u'lláh uses parable and narrative in his writings, but his style is generally eclectic, switching from one form to another and sometimes quoting and paraphrasing other authors, traditional stories, and earlier writings of his own. In the Seven Valleys, for example, Bahá'u'lláh retells briefly an episode from the well-known story of Layla and Majnun. In the same work, he also shows great familiarity with the writings of various mystics such as Farídu'd-Dín 'Attár, Jalálu'd-Dín Rúmí, Shaykh Abú Ismá'íl 'Abdu'lláh Ansárí, and others.[1]

Bahá'u'lláh's dramatic use of symbolism is a facet of the hyperbolic style so common to Near-Eastern literature and so appropriate to the mystic's attempts to describe the quest to attain the presence of God. His message is cast in definitives and superlatives intended to add a passionate emphasis to his message and often to heighten the sense of pathos.[2] This tendency is sufficiently extreme to warn informed readers to be weary of literalism. This is a language of the heart.

Without knowledge of the various ancient scriptural stories to which Bahá'u'lláh is alluding, the Tablet would appear far more cryptic than it is.

Bahá'u'lláh said that sacred writings often have many meanings, but there is no reason to confuse this with the idea that they can have arbitrary meaning. With that in mind, it is useful to have some knowledge of the symbolism used in the Tablet's composition.

The Tablet of the Holy Mariner contains numerous symbols in the form of people, places, objects, and actions. All of these symbols, however, fall within basic groups with known scriptural antecedents. The basic symbols used by Bahá'u'lláh to construct his narrative of the Holy Mariner were well known to his audience when the Tablet was first read in 1863. With these symbols, he fashions a cosmological order with spatial and physical symbols to create a recognizable but imaginative vision of the spiritual universe—a stage on which he can unfold a drama involving seekers, divine virtues, the path to divinity, the struggle between faithfulness and pride, and more. It is a stage where the realities of human nature and the potentialities of the soul for waywardness or liberation are revealed. With this overall construction, a drama comes together to convey mystical and theological teachings, moral guidance, and prophecies of future events.

The basic symbols he used for this vision originate from a long heritage. They begin with the Hebrew scriptures and then undergo further evolution in folklore, and later in Christian and Islamic sources, as well as in the writings of the Báb, and in the poetry of the mystics.[3] Yet, to the modern reader raised in a secular society, these symbols may only be recollected vaguely and their rich theological associations completely unknown. To better appreciate the Tablet it will be helpful to first reintroduce some of these symbols and their subtler aspects. It is through the use of a shared language and symbolism that the greatest ability to communicate is achieved. Had Bahá'u'lláh used unfamiliar symbols and literary forms, his audience would have had to struggle to comprehend even the most basic aspects of his message. Bahá'u'lláh, like the Sufi poets, did not just recount stories that recall verbatim their original version, but rather subtly refashioned them to reveal a new significance to his audience. It is not just the symbols themselves that have importance, the new retelling must also be appreciated. The more familiar the listener is with the original symbols, the easier it is to detect the nuances of the new message.

Many of the symbols in the Tablet of the Holy Mariner are derived from five basic symbolic narratives which have antecedents in Jewish tradition and scripture. These are listed in the table on page 45.

Since each of these symbols is already rich with associations, their use allowed Bahá'u'lláh to put volumes of meaning into concise expressions. In some cases, there are aspects of the original symbols that are not expressed openly in the Tablet, but

Main symbols and scriptural antecedents

Symbol	Scripture
1. The ark of eternity	Noah's ark: See Qur'an 11:36–49, 26:119, and Genesis, chapters 6–8 Ark of the covenant: See Exodus 25:10–22, 40:1–38.
2. The expulsion of the angels Also related to this symbolism: The guardian angels The angelic concourse	The fall of Iblís or Lucifer: See Isaiah 14:12–15, Qur'an 2:32; 38:74–78. Cherubim: See Qur'an 2:97–98, 50:17–18, Genesis 3:24, Exodus 25:18–22, and Psalm 91:11. The hosts of heaven: For examples, see Qur'an 35:1, 42:5, 79:1–5; Deuteronomy 4:19, 1 Kings 22:19, Nehemiah 9:6.
3. The flame within the deathless tree	The Sinai episode in the Book of Exodus, in particular, the burning bush encountered by Moses. See Qur'an 27:7–14, 28:29–32. For parallel in Bible see Exodus, chapter 3 and 4:6–7. See also Genesis 3:2–4, Revelation 22:2.
4. The Maid of Heaven	The feminine personification of wisdom: Proverbs 9:1–6 and especially the Apocryphal books of The Wisdom of Solomon, chapters 6–10 and Ecclesiasticus, chapters 1, 4:11–19, 6:18–31, and 24.
5. The robe and fragrance of the Beloved Youth	The story of Joseph: Qur'an 12:4–101. For parallel in Bible, see Genesis, chapters 37–48.

which contain keys to understanding the meaning. For example, the motive of jealousy and the act of betrayal are nowhere stated explicitly in the Tablet, but in the quranic and biblical account of the fall of the angels (and in particular the angel Lucifer), pride and jealousy are major aspects of the accounts. Anyone familiar with these accounts would probably have recognized the underlying suggestion in Bahá'u'lláh's words.

The Ark of Eternity

The Tablet of the Holy Mariner begins with the Mariner inviting the angelic spirits to enter an ark. He then embarks on a journey across the seas to the Mountain of God. This is the classic mystical symbolism of the soul's journey. It is common in ancient moral literature and mystical writings to describe the development of the soul and its progress to God as a journey or pilgrimage. Sometimes it is a sea-faring journey, as in Homer's Odyssey; or a journey through the heavens, as in the stories of the night journey of Muḥammad (the *mi'ráj*), or in Dante's *Divine Comedy*. In Jewish literature, the metaphor of a sea-faring journey is expressed well in the Fourth Book of Maccabees.[4] In the Báb's writings, he uses the metaphor of *"sailing upon the sea of God's Names,"* and *"sailing upon the sea of creation,"* to delineate different types of spiritual understanding.[5] Bahá'u'lláh's earlier work, the Book of Certitude, opens with a type of thesis statement upon which the first part of the book is an exposition. This opening passage stresses the importance of detachment while using a sea-faring journey as a metaphor: *"No man shall attain the shores of the ocean of true understanding except he be detached from all that is in heaven and on earth."*[6]

In the Tablet of the Holy Mariner, Bahá'u'lláh begins his description of the soul's journey using symbolism suggesting the story of Noah's ark, a popular subject of Islamic folklore and poetry.[7] However, the purpose here is not the salvation of the animal kingdom, or of just the solitary seeker. Rather, the emphasis is on the religious community, an idea indicated by the plural term "dwellers therein." Bahá'u'lláh refers to the ark as the ark "of eternity" to signify that the ark is a universal and timeless archetype. Beyond being a means of preservation, like the symbolic ark described in the story of Noah, the eternal ark is a means of transportation—transporting souls to higher consciousness. The waters represent the perils of the journey and can signify anything that might overwhelm the seeker: doctrinal complexities, the interpretation of scripture, the temptations of life, adversaries in the community, or other spiritual tests. The Mariner is a type of Noah in the quranic sense, a prophetic warner and savior giving refuge to God's creatures. He is the provider of refuge and safe passage in perilous circumstances.

In the story of Noah, the ark is a rudderless boat that serves as a lifeboat, and in the end it comes to rest on a mountain. In Bahá'u'lláh's version, this imagery is fused with the symbolism of Moses' encounter with the burning bush near Mount Sinai. This is first indicated by the fact that the ark sails to the shore of the crimson seas, symbolism suggesting the Red Sea in the Qur'an and book of Exodus (v. 6). In the tale, as told by Bahá'u'lláh, the ark stops at the shore of the crimson seas, where the dwellers either disembark and journey to the burning Bush, or they are mystically carried there where they then disembark (see verses 12 and 13). In a later work, Bahá'u'lláh refers to a crimson ark and says: *"Verily, it passeth over land and sea."*[8] If brought together, these nuances of the symbolism, further suggest the spiritual reality of the ark. However one reads this symbolism, the Ark appears as a reality that preserves seekers wherever they are in this world and carries them on their journey to the heights of spirituality.

In the biblical and quranic narrative, entering the sacred land of Mount Sinai required passing through the Red Sea. In a mystical sense, this route with its miraculous associations, is the only route that leads to the holy mountain. The waters can have many symbolic meanings. They can represent the Revelation of God, an ocean containing impenetrable depths or the unity of God upon which one sails but does not encompass. It can also represent the turmoils and perils of life, or contending opinions about the meaning of scripture, as in the story of Jesus' calming the stormy sea.[9]

In the Báb's first book, an unconventional commentary on the Qur'an's Surih of Joseph, he referred to crimson-colored *"Arks of ruby . . . wherein none shall sail but the people of Bahá (glory)."*[10] The existence of this reference must have suggested to the Bábís present in Baghdad in 1863, the possibility that the holy Mariner referred to Bahá'u'lláh. In a later work, Bahá'u'lláh identifies explicitly the crimson Ark mentioned in the Báb's commentary with the *"people of Bahá."*[11]

The Expulsion of the Angels

The Tablet of the Holy Mariner makes numerous references to celestial beings. In the opening verse the Celestial Concourse (v. 1) is mentioned and referred to repeatedly throughout the Tablet (v. 26, 49, and 52). Bahá'u'lláh also refers to angelic spirits (v. 3), guardian angels (v. 22), the inmates of the chambers of Paradise (v. 37), and the maids of heaven (v. 25, 33, 49, 55). The Tablet has a very hierarchal cosmographical symbolism, and the celestial beings are to a lesser extent also arranged in a hierarchal structure. There are, for example, various plains, or spheres, through which the faithful ascend and which are inhabited by celestial and angelic beings. The Maid of Heaven, a female personification of wisdom, appears to occupy the highest position. The Tablet provides, however, no clear picture of the hierarchy of angels; rather they all occupy different roles or stations.[12] The guardian angels, for example, suggest the Cherubim who guard the entrance to paradise[13] and whose image is put on the Ark of the Testimony in the Holy of Holies.[14] The initial drama in the midst of these heavenly hosts is the expulsion of the angelic persons who seek to ascend beyond the stations ordained by virtue of their own natures (v. 19–22). In Bahá'u'lláh's writings, angels refer to saintly people whether in this world or the next—and most ideally to *"holy beings"* who *"have sanctified themselves from every human limitation, have become endowed with the attributes of the spiritual."*[15]

The characteristics of this drama reflect the ancient account of the rebellion and expulsion of Lucifer. The faithful on earth—those who enter the ark—are called "angelic spirits," but once they have tried to ascend too high they are cast out by a meteor and returned to earth by guardian angels. Once the angelic spirits are cast out, they are, of course, "fallen" angels like "Lucifer" (from the Latin translation of the Hebrew, which literally means to give off light, and often equated with the morning star, or daystar). He's described in the Book of Isaiah and identified with Satan in Jewish, Christian, and Islamic traditions.[16]

Traditionally, the term *satan* is equated with Lucifer and used in biblical literature to signify an adversary of God. This can be used either in a singular or plural sense. That is, anyone could be a satan, since everyone has the potential to be an adversary to what is right and good. In the biblical account most expressive of this theme, Lucifer is cast out because of his pride implicit in his desire to *"scale the heavens; higher than the stars of God"* and *"rival the Most High."*[17] This theme of pride and jealousy is also central to descriptions in the Qur'an and in the writings of the Báb. However, in the Tablet of the Holy Mariner Bahá'u'lláh never explicitly mentions Satan, pride, jealousy, or even opposition. The angels are cast out because they *"desire"* to reach a station which God has ordained to be above them. Pride and jealousy are, rather inferred by the broader connotations inherent in the traditional symbolism. The station desired is the station conferred on one person only, the spiritual guide signified in the Tablet by both the Mariner and the Youth. Jealousy is implied in the act of rivaling the true possessor of this divine station.

In the book of Isaiah, Lucifer wishes to be like God, which means that Godhood is the station sought after. In the quranic version, God creates Adam perfect and innocent and commands all the angels to pay homage to him. Filled with pride, Satan wants to be worshiped like Adam and refuses to bow down. Why would God ask the angels to bow down before Adam? This question is answered indirectly in the Báb's writings:

> *When God created the Remembrance [Adam] He presented Him to the assemblage of all created beings upon the altar of His Will. Thereupon the concourse of the angels bowed low in adoration to God, the Peerless, the Incomparable; while Satan waxed proud, refusing to submit to His Remembrance; hence he is identified in the Book of God as the arrogant one and the accursed.*[18]

The station of Adam can be best appreciated in light of the Bahá'í teachings concerning Manifestations of God. In Bábí and Bahá'í theology, God is unknowable both in this world and the next, except through God's Manifestations. All things manifest God to a limited degree, while human being possess the potential to manifest God to the greatest degree. Among human beings, persons such as Moses, Jesus, Muḥammad, Buddha, the Báb, and Bahá'u'lláh are regarded as the supreme Manifestations of God. It is through them that God's will is revealed to humankind. They subordinate their own wills to such an extent that all that can be seen in them is God's will. Bahá'u'lláh describes this station *"the station in which one dieth to himself and liveth in God."*[19] For this reason they speak from the point of view of God's voice and refer to their words as the words of God.[20] History shows that it is rare for persons occupying this spiritual station to appear.[21] Of all the manifestations of God that appear in this world, Bahá'u'lláh says this exalted station is the most supreme Manifestation of God that ever takes place.

This is not the same as God appearing literally, since God is too transcendent to be revealed in totality or essence. But rather it is a station that is *likened* to the presence of God. Whosoever attains the presence of these holy and supreme Manifestations in effect attains the presence of God.[22] The attainment of God's presence referred to in the scriptures, such as on the Day of Resurrection, refers outwardly to attaining to the presence of these historic persons. More broadly one enters the presences of God through recognition of God's Manifestation in the age in which the Manifestation appears and adherence to the Manifestation's teachings. While the Manifestations may take up different missions in this world, the light reflected in them comes from one Source, and for this reason the eternal logos, the pre-existent Muḥammadan light, the universal Buddhahood, are also all one. None is greater or different in nature than the other. Or as explained by

Bahá'u'lláh: *"in the eyes of them that are initiated into the mysteries of divine wisdom, all their utterances are in reality but the expressions of one Truth."*[23]

Adam is included in this pantheon of divine Manifestations, signifying symbolically the first Manifestation of God in the world of creation.[24] With this in mind, the mental picture of the angels sitting together with God looking down on Adam is essentially inaccurate from the point of view of Bábí symbolism. Even the angels are unable to ascend to the actual throne of God. Therefore, when God created Adam, Adam was God's Manifestation in the world of creation. The perfect Adam was the vicegerent of God, the channel through whom even the angels would need to turn in lieu of attaining the presence of God. When the angels bowed before Adam, they were in effect actually bowing before God. Referring to the apocalyptic symbolism of the Day of Judgment, when God is said to appear, the Báb writes:

> *For on that Day all men will be brought before God and will attain His Presence; which meaneth appearance before Him Who is the Tree of divine Reality and attainment unto His presence; inasmuch as it is not possible to appear before the Most Holy Essence of God, nor is it conceivable to seek reunion with Him. That which is feasible in the matter of appearance before Him [God] and of meeting Him is attainment unto the Primal Tree [the Manifestation of God].*[25]

In Bahá'u'lláh's writings, Adam also signifies the perfect human being, and as such represents the presence of God on earth—as do all God's Manifestations, such as Noah, Moses, Buddha, Jesus, Muḥammad, and so on. From this point of view, the Tablet of the Holy Mariner uses the symbolism of the expulsion of the angels to represent the desire of people to claim to be more than they really are. This especially refers to those who claim to possess the authority of God, when in fact they are refusing to submit to the will of God in their own lives. In this sense, it is the same as one who desires to be like Jesus or any other Manifestation of God, that is, to be treated like them while failing to possess their spiritual station and divinity. The wise person is the one who knows his or her true station. Rúmí writes:

> Since you are not a prophet, follow the Way! . . .
> Since you are not a sultan, be a subject! Since you are not the captain, take not yourself the helm! . . .

> Listen to the text, Be silent!, and be silent! Since you have not become God's tongue, be an ear![26]

Although the seeker should *aspire* to be like Jesus, to imagine or claim that one possesses such a great station and that others should follow you is a grievous affliction. To oppose the Manifestations of God in an effort to claim such supremacy for one's own self is the ultimate of pride and vainglorious ambition. The sincere seeker must be free from this impulse. Bahá'u'lláh writes:

> *Wherefore must the veils of the satanic self be burned away at the fire of love, that the spirit may be purified and cleansed and thus may know the station of the Lord of the Worlds.*[27]

The Bahá'í historical interpretation of the Tablet of the Holy Mariner sees the "desired" station as that station occupied by Bahá'u'lláh and coveted by his half-brother Mírzá Yahyá. The spiritual *authority* inherent in such a station can also be conferred on others, even as Jesus conferred authority on his apostle Saint Peter.[28] Bahá'u'lláh appointed his saintly son 'Abdu'l-Bahá to be his successor and also the sole authoritative interpreter of his writings.[29] Although this did not make 'Abdu'l-Bahá a supreme Manifestation of God like Christ or Bahá'u'lláh, it did confer on him Bahá'u'lláh's authority. This succession of divine authority was the covenant by which Bahá'u'lláh sought to safeguard the unity and spiritual well being of his followers.

In this way, 'Abdu'l-Bahá occupied a unique station which only he could possess. His authority was further extended when he appointed his grandson, Shoghi Effendi, as his successor. Those who sought to usurp this unique station created a pattern of rebellion that represents the continuation of the original archetype of rebellion described in the Tablet of the Holy Mariner. This is why the Tablet has a continuing historical significance to the Bahá'í community as it tries to preserve its unity and protect its spiritual life from the strife and confusion of sectarianism.

The overall symbolism of fallen angels is rooted in a metaphorical understanding of physical reality. Since ancient times, the stars have been seen as a means of navigation. For this reason, the righteous sages and saints have been likened to stars, celestial guides for the seeker to follow. This is reflected in the Book of Daniel which states that *"those who have instructed many in uprightness"* will shine *"as bright as stars for all eternity."*[30] When the righteous cease to follow the right path they are like falling stars or meteors, an interpretation given by Bahá'u'lláh to Jesus' prophecy that the stars will fall from heaven before the last days.³¹ This role of the stars is the likely root of the meteor symbolism. In the Qur'an this symbolism of the meteor or shooting star casting out evil spirits and guarding heaven recurs in several passages.³² The twelfth-century Persian poet Anvarí writes of God giving "the stars the power of throwing [meteors] at devils."³³

The act of casting out has significance to the spiritual life and to people seeking communion with God. The sages have always understood that association with immoral and corrupt souls may cause the seeker to stumble and fall off the path of God.³⁴ The enlightened are urged to be guides and show love to the wayward, but to avoid any intimacy and companionship that might cause their waywardness to influence them. When Bahá'u'lláh outlines the steps a seeker should take to arrive at the city of God, he writes: *"He should treasure the companionship of those that have renounced the world, and regard avoidance of boastful and worldly people a precious benefit. . . . With all his heart should the seeker avoid fellowship with evil doers, and pray for the remission of their sins."*³⁵

To help insure the unity of the Bahá'í community, this teaching is also reflected in the instruction to avoid companionship with persons who are using religion to gain personal power, especially those who seek to divide the community and break with the covenant established by Bahá'u'lláh. The point is not that people should only associate with saints, even if such persons were easy to find. Rather, it is simply wiser and more conducive to spiritual growth to seek the company of those who share spiritual aspirations. Avoidance not only protects, it neutralizes the source of the problem. The creation of a spiritual community creates both the blessings of spiritual companionship and support, as well as the tests of trials that come from those who seek to gain power and exalt themselves within the community. As long as people come together to combine their powers for the betterment of others, there will be people who seek to take control of that power at whatever level they can to enhance their own position and prestige in this world. Such spiritual tests are always greater than the tests that come from those outside the community. For that reason, the archetypal symbolism in the Tablet of the Holy Mariner will never cease to be relevant to seekers on the path to God.

The Deathless Tree
In the Tablet of the Holy Mariner, the passengers of the ark (v. 7) are taken to a snow-white spot (v. 14), likely to be the valley of Ṭuwá³⁶ mentioned in the Qur'an at the base of Mount Sinai. There they encounter the beauty of the Lord in a burning Tree (v. 8). These symbolic features suggest the description of Moses'

encounter with the burning bush described in the Book of Exodus and in the Qur'an. The place is where God spoke to Moses, the base of the Mountain where the Torah would be revealed later. This is made more apparent by the reference to the glory—signifying splendor, light, and presence—of Moses circling the sacred Tree with the everlasting hosts. The station wherein *"the Hand of God was drawn forth from His bosom of Grandeur"* is likewise a reference to the Sinai episode.[37]

Bahá'u'lláh's retelling of the Sinai episode, however, is from a heightened mystical point of view. The emphasis is on disclosing the divinity of Moses to create an equation between Moses and the presence of God. In this sense, it is not the historical Moses, but rather the eternal inmost reality—the Logos, the pre-existent Sophia, the Word, the Spirit of God—that is Moses and all the Manifestations of God. In this sense, no distinction is made between the "Lord" (v. 8) and Moses (v. 10, 11). In verse 8, the Lord's presence is indicated by the flame within the Tree; and in verse 10, the glory of Moses is circling the Tree. Since "glory" itself indicates theologically the light and presence of God, the flame and the glory are essentially one.

This theology is evident particularly in Bahá'u'lláh's retelling of the trial of Moses' hand seen in the Tablet of the Holy Mariner (v. 11). In the biblical version, Moses has doubts and God provides a series of evidences of His total sovereignty. In this instance, Moses is told to put his hand in his garment and then bring it out. When he does this his hand is covered with leprosy. God then tells him to put his hand back in and withdraw it again. This time Moses' hand is restored. Bahá'u'lláh's version is told very differently using hyperbolic imagery. It is not Moses' hand, but rather the "Hand of God" that is drawn forth, as if to say, that Moses's own mortal hand was in itself no more than the hand of a leper (in comparison with the hand of God). God now in effect transforms Moses' hand into His own hand. All of these significances come together to suggest that the purpose of the ark's journey is to enable its passengers to attain the presence of God, to realize the establishment of a new covenant. This is the destination of those who enter the ark.

The correlations between the symbolism in the Tablet of the Holy Mariner and the Sinai episode also suggest other theological themes. In the biblical and traditional account of the Sinai episode, Moses makes a request to see God, there is a symbolic disclosure of God's Name, and the Torah, or law of God, is revealed. Each of these features is likely to be a source of underlying meaning for Bahá'u'lláh's message in the Tablet. In many theological traditions, it is understood that it is impossible to see God directly; but through knowledge of, and obedience to God's will, a seeker can attain (so to speak) the presence of God. On Mount Sinai, Moses asked God: *"Please show me Your glory"*[38] also translated as *"let me behold Your Presence."*[39] God tells Moses that he cannot see His full glory, but that He will allow him to see a trace of it.[40] In the Qur'an, the Sinai episode is retold with a more forceful use of symbolism to convey this idea of disclosure:

> *And when Moses came to Our appointed time and his Lord spoke with him, he said, "Oh my Lord, show me, that I may behold Thee!" Said He, "Thou shalt not see Me; but behold the mountain—if it stays fast in its place, then thou shalt see Me." And when his Lord revealed Him to the mountain He made it crumble to dust; and Moses fell down swooning.*[41]

This account provides a possible clue to one of the more enigmatic verses in the Tablet of the Holy Mariner. In verse 12, Bahá'u'lláh refers to the ark of the Cause remaining motionless *"even though to its dwellers be declared all divine attributes."* Since the Revelation of God in His totality is so overpowering that it crushes the mountain, it is possible that this verse is speaking of a disclosure of God which, although very great, can still be experienced. This disclosure is likely to be God in the person of His Manifestations, that is, persons such as Moses, Christ, Muḥammad, and Bahá'u'lláh. One can see the attributes of God in them without being overwhelmed and crushed by the experience.

In the Tablet of the Holy Mariner, once the dwellers in the ark reach the mountain base they are taught a hidden knowledge that then enables them to ascend to heaven. The text refers to this knowledge as, *"that which we [God, and symbolically, Sophia and the angel Gabriel] have taught thee [the Mariner/Bahá'u'lláh] behind the mystic veil"* (v. 13). In Jewish lore, it is the secret knowledge of the hidden Name of God that enables the angels to ascend to heaven.[42] This hidden knowledge can be signified succinctly as the Name of God. In this Tablet, one meaning would clearly be the understanding of the divine significance of the names "the Báb" and "Bahá'u'lláh." In Bahá'í theology, the name of the Manifestation, in whichever age the Manifestation appears, is equated with the "Greatest Name," the hidden unutterable and unknowable Name of God.

While on Mount Sinai, Moses asked God, *"When I come to the Israelites and say to them, 'The God of your fathers has sent me to you,' and they say to me, 'What is His name?' what shall I say to them?"*[43] God answers Moses saying *"Ehyeh-Asher-Ehyeh,"* and continued, *"Thus you shall say to the Israelites, 'Ehyeh-Asher-Ehyeh sent me to* you.'"⁴⁴ The meaning of the Hebrew phrase *"Ehyeh-Asher-Ehyeh"* is of uncertain origin, but has been translated as *"I am Who I am."* In several instances, Jesus identifies himself with God by making connections between his reality and this Sinai episode. In one example, Jesus said *"Your father Abraham rejoiced to think that he would see my Day, he saw it and was glad."*⁴⁵ Here Jesus suggests that he and Abraham were present together. When those listening to Jesus objected, Jesus uses the Sinai episode to reinforce the same point, saying *"In all truth I tell you, before Abraham ever was, I am."*⁴⁶ When Jesus said, *"before Abraham was, I am,"* He appears to be indicating that his voice is none other than the same Voice of God which Moses heard on Mount Sinai. That is, the same eternal God that existed before Abraham is now speaking through Christ. *"I am Who I am"* suggests the self-evident proof of God's divinity as it is manifested to the world. *"The proof of the sun is the light thereof, which shineth and envelopeth all things."*⁴⁷

In the Báb's writings there are also statements very similar to Christ's words. The Báb writes, *"I am the Flame of that supernal Light that glowed upon Sinai in the gladsome Spot, and lay concealed in the midst of the Burning Bush."*⁴⁸ In this verse the Báb identifies himself with the flame of the Burning Bush itself, but in other passages he speaks of the Burning Bush entrusting him with a mission. This is parallel to the biblical account wherein Moses is entrusted with a mission from the Burning Bush: *"Give ear unto God's holy Voice proclaimed by this Arabian Youth [the Báb] Whom the Almighty hath graciously chosen for His Own Self. He is indeed none other than the True One, Whom God hath entrusted with this Mission from the midst of the Burning Bush."*⁴⁹ In this passage, the Báb has become a new Moses. In another passage the Báb uses the same metaphor in the Qur'an when he writes: *"Indeed We conversed with Moses by the leave of God from the midst of the Burning Bush in the Sinai and revealed an infinitesimal glimmer of Thy Light upon the Mystic Mount and its dwellers, whereupon the Mount shook to its foundations and was crushed into dust."*⁵⁰ Similarly Bahá'u'lláh says that people today are hearing from him what Moses *"heard upon the Sinai of divine knowledge."*⁵¹ By this, he is not asserting that it was him in person who spoke to Moses, but rather that the voice in the Burning Bush is the same Spirit of God that now speaks through him.

God's response to Moses' request to know God's identity, does not come in the form of a specific *name*. Bahá'u'lláh writes that God is *"He Who can neither be named, nor described."*⁵² In scripture, the term *name*, and especially with reference to God, was a way of signifying the Reality of God. The term *name* was not used in a way equivalent to its modern usage.⁵³ In one of his prayers, Bahá'u'lláh declares that the "Name" of God is a name *"which no scroll can bear, which no heart* can imagine and no tongue can utter—a Name which will remain concealed so long as Thine own Essence is hidden, and will be glorified so long as Thine own Being is extolled."⁵⁴ Nevertheless, even as the Manifestation signifies God "the Hidden" on earth, the Manifestation's name signifies God's hidden name. This is reflected in the New Testament when it is said that Christ appeared in God's greatest name. Saint Paul says that God gave Jesus "the name which is above all other names, so that *all beings* in the heavens, on earth and in the underworld *should bend the knee* at the name of Jesus and that *every tongue should acknowledge* Jesus Christ as Lord, to the glory of God the Father."⁵⁵ Saint Peter, likewise said, "for of all the names in the world given to men, this is the only one by which we can be saved."⁵⁶ Jesus himself proclaims, *"I have revealed your name."*⁵⁷

In the theology of Bahá'u'lláh, these same truths are applicable to all Manifestations of God in whatever age they appear, whether the name be "Buddha," "Muḥammad," "Jesus," or the name of any other Manifestation of God. Bahá'u'lláh writes: *"These Prophets and chosen Ones of God are the recipients and revealers of all the unchangeable attributes and names of God. They are the mirrors that truly and faithfully reflect the light of God. Whatsoever is applicable to them is in reality applicable to God, Himself, Who is both the Visible and the Invisible."*⁵⁸ Bahá'u'lláh explains that all the Messengers of God are *"one person, one soul, one spirit, one being, one revelation. They are all the manifestation of the 'Beginning' and the 'End,' the 'First' and the 'Last,' the 'Seen' and the 'Hidden'—all of which pertain to Him Who is the Innermost Spirit of Spirits and Eternal Essence of Essences."*⁵⁹ Knowing the Greatest Name of God, which enables the seeker to ascend to heaven, is the same as drawing close to God through the knowledge of God's Messengers.

As well as being the disclosure of God's name, the Burning Bush is a symbol that can signify many other spiritual truths. The tree, which connects heaven and earth by virtue of the fact that it has roots in the ground and branches in the sky, has always had important symbolic significance. The tree represents the growth potentiality of God's kingdom, the seasonal renewal of God's disclosure, a place of shelter, a source of sustenance, a place of meeting, a living presence. Because the Burning Bush signified the means by which God spoke to the world, this humble Bush, as distinguished from a tree, can be likened to the seemingly insignificant Israelite nation through which God also spoke to the world. That is, God chose an oppressed people through which to demonstrate His power over the great nations of the world, signified by the Egyptian empire.

Nevertheless, this is only one way that such a symbol can be interpreted. In some passages, Bahá'u'lláh speaks of the mystical *"Tree"* that *"belongeth neither to the*

East nor to the West."[60] In Bahá'u'lláh's writings He also directly identifies the Prophet Moses with the Reality symbolized by the Burning Bush when he says *"Pharaoh and his people"* exerted *"their utmost endeavour to extinguish with the waters of falsehood and denial the fire of that sacred Tree."*[61] Since neither the Pharaoh nor his people ever reached Mount Sinai, it is clear that this is poetic license—the fire of that sacred Tree which they sought to extinguish is none other than the divine reality of Moses himself, the eternal light of God.

Christ stated that the Kingdom of God was like *"a mustard seed which a man took and threw into his garden: it grew and became a tree, and the birds of the air sheltered in its branches."*[62] One way of understanding this tree is to think of the gardener as God who planted the seed at the beginning of humankind's spiritual history. The Kingdom of God in the time of Moses grew to be like a small bush but in later ages it became a great tree. Throughout the ages, God sends Prophets and inspired saints who water this tree of life. This tree, in its full growth, was first visualized in the original paradise of God, the garden of Eden. Its archetypal reality is then presented again in the Book of Revelation in a description of the restored Paradise of God. Through sanctification, Bahá'u'lláh writes that the seeker can re-enter this original paradise, and attain the presence of God in the shade of this Tree:

> *Have ye forgotten that true and radiant morn, when in those hallowed and blessed surroundings ye were all gathered in My presence beneath the shade of the tree of life, which is planted in the all-glorious paradise? Awe-struck ye listened as I gave utterance to these three most holy words: O friends! Prefer not your will to Mine, never desire that which I have not desired for you, and approach Me not with lifeless hearts, defiled with worldly desires and cravings. Would ye but sanctify your souls, ye would at this present hour recall that place and those surroundings, and the truth of My utterance should be made evident unto all of you.*[63]

With regard to sanctification and purification, Bahá'u'lláh's writings describe a station wherein the flame appears as the station *"wherein the embodiments of His Cause cleansed themselves of self and passion"* (v. 7–12). This juxtaposition of fire and purification has many parallels in sacred literature. In Christianity, for example, the Gospel speaks of baptism by the Holy Spirit and by fire.[64] In many passages, Bahá'u'lláh uses the term "fire" or "flame" as a symbol for the "fire of love" that purifies and cleanses the spirit.[65]

The Burning Bush and the revelation of the Law; the Tree of Life situated in paradise with the original command not to eat of its fruit; the purification and sanctification that occurs in the station where the flame appears; the hidden knowledge that enables the seekers to ascend into heaven—all these symbols of renunciation, obedience to God's will, and illumination through knowledge of God's attributes, converge to form a message of how to ascend to the presence of God, which is the ultimate aim of the mystic's quest.

The Heavenly Maidens

In the Tablet of the Holy Mariner, the Maid of Heaven is described as a luminous being, flooding both heaven and earth with her light (v. 27–28), a light that awakens people in their graves (v. 29). She is the conveyer of a message that is juxtaposed against the backdrop of the expulsion of the angels. That message concerns the prerequisite for admittance into the highest heaven (v. 30–32). Following this message, she calls upon one of her handmaidens and instructs her to descend into the world and search for faithful souls (v. 33–38). The search is ordered so that the inhabitants of the celestial realm may come down and pay homage to the faithful.

The symbolism of a heavenly realm populated by celestial inhabitants with male and female genders is common to most religious traditions. Celestial maidens pervade the Qur'an.[66] But Bahá'u'lláh's use of feminine personifications in a hierarchal structure is more characteristic of Buddhist and Jewish symbolism than the descriptions found in the Qur'an. Bahá'u'lláh first introduces the singular figure of the Maid of Heaven, and she then calls on *"one maiden from her handmaidens"* (v. 33). Although this imagery is similar to imagery in the popular ta'ziyah performances mentioned previously, Bahá'u'lláh's imagery also correlates well with a description found in the Book of Proverbs. The Tablet of the Holy Mariner contains characteristics that suggest, as do some other writings by Bahá'u'lláh, the use of symbolism based more directly on Judaic texts than on the Qur'an, though these sources may be mediated through Islamic texts other than the Qur'an.[67]

The Maid of Heaven is such an example. Although this type of symbolism exists in many ancient writings, Bahá'u'lláh's Maid of Heaven is a personification very much like that found in Jewish wisdom literature. As in the Tablet of the Holy Mariner, the Book of Proverbs describes Wisdom sending out her handmaidens to search for the faithful. In the Book of Proverbs reference to the personification of Wisdom is brief and relatively undescriptive. The text focuses on a description of Wisdom as preparing a feast in heaven for the faithful and the handmaidens are sent out to gather the guests. Later writings, however, provide a fuller expansion of the symbolism, such as in the apocryphal books the Wisdom of Solomon and Ecclesiaticus. Wisdom, in the Apocryphal texts (Greek, *Sophia*), is described as a pre-existent reality, the source of creation, an emissary of God who appears to the saints and prophets throughout history in their hour of trial. She is associated with the Law of God and sought after by the wisest of people. This type of description which identifies her as the pre-existent Logos or Spirit of God is contained in the writings of Bahá'u'lláh.[68] This feminine imagery is a dominant symbol used in connection with Bahá'u'lláh's own theophanic experience. In his Súratu'l-Haykal (the Súrih of the Temple), Bahá'u'lláh writes a passage that contains a description of a maiden very similar to the description in the Tablet of the Holy Mariner:

> *While engulfed in tribulations I heard a most wondrous, a most sweet voice, calling above My head. Turning My face, I beheld a Maiden—the embodiment of the remembrance of the name of My Lord—suspended in the air before Me. So rejoiced was she in her very soul that her countenance shone with the ornament of the good-pleasure of God, and her cheeks glowed with the brightness of the All-Merciful. Betwixt earth and heaven she was raising a call which captivated the hearts and minds of men. She was imparting to both My inward and outer being tidings which rejoiced My soul, and the souls of God's honored servants. Pointing with her finger unto My head, she addressed all who are in heaven and all who are on earth, saying: 'By God! This is the Best-Beloved of the worlds, and yet ye comprehend not. This is the Beauty of God amongst you, and the power of His sovereignty within you, could ye but understand. This is the Mystery of God and His Treasure, the Cause of God and His glory unto all who are in the kingdoms of Revelation and of creation, if ye be of them that perceive.'"*[69]

This theophanic description of the Maiden is in a later work connected with his imprisonment in the Síyáh-Chál in 1852, and identified directly with Wisdom. In the Words of Paradise, Bahá'u'lláh writes: *"Wisdom is God's emissary and the revealer of His Name the Omniscient . . . thanks to its educating influence earthly beings have become imbued with a gemlike spirit which outshineth the heaven. In the city of justice it is the unrivaled Speaker Who, in the year nine, illumined the world with the joyful tidings of this Revelation."*[70] The city of justice is the capital of Persia, Tehran;

and the year "nine" is 1269 of the Islamic calendar. The year nine had special significance to the Bábís. The description of Wisdom actively mediating the Revelation of God to holy souls and prophets reflects the words of the Book of Wisdom, *"she renews the world, and generation after generation, passing into holy souls, she makes them into God's friends and prophets."*[71]

In the Qur'an the maids of heaven are the brides of the faithful in this life. *"For the righteous is a beautiful place of (final) return,"* an *"eternal home"* with *"companions pure (and holy),"* *"chaste women restraining their glances, (companions) of equal age,"* *"virgin-pure (and undefiled),"* whom *"no man or Jinn before them has touched"* *"fair (companions), good and beautiful,"* *"with beautiful, big, and lustrous eyes,"* *"like unto Pearls well-guarded,"* *"a reward for the deeds of their past life,"* *"dressed in fine silk and rich brocade, they will face each other,"* in *"pavilions,"* *"reclining on green cushions and rich carpets of beauty."*[72] In Bahá'u'lláh's Book of Certitude, these maids of heaven (Arabic, *húrís*) are given a metaphorical meaning signifying spiritual understanding or truth. The virginity of the *húrís*, expounded in Islamic tradition, is used by Bahá'u'lláh to symbolize the untouched or undiscovered nature of the truth the maidens personify (or signify). Bahá'u'lláh writes:

> *Notwithstanding all that We have mentioned, how innumerable are the pearls which have remained unpierced in the shell of Our heart! How many the húrís of inner meaning that are as yet concealed within the chambers of divine wisdom! None hath yet approached them;—húrís, "whom no man nor spirit hath touched before."*[73] *Notwithstanding all that hath been said, it seemeth as if not one letter of Our purpose hath been uttered, nor a single sign divulged concerning Our object. When will a faithful seeker be found who will don the garb of pilgrimage, attain the Ka'bih of the heart's desire, and, without ear or tongue, discover the mysteries of divine utterance?*[74]

This use of symbolism provides important insights into the Tablet of the Holy Mariner. The Maid of Heaven sends her handmaiden into the world to seek out faithful seekers so that the inmates of paradise can then pay homage to them. In this case, no gender is indicated with regard to the inmates of paradise or the faithful on earth. In one sense, these inhabitants can represent hidden insights and spiritual virtues. Those who follow the spiritual path are united with these divine realities—a celestial marriage. In another sense, the maidens who appear at the tragic ending of the Tablet represent the apprehension of previously unknown insights.

SYMBOLISM

The Exiled Youth

In the Tablet of the Holy Mariner, the Maid of Heaven declares that only those who love the "Arabian Youth" can ascend into the highest heaven (v. 31–32). She then calls upon one of her handmaidens to descend into the world and search for those from whose robes the fragrance of the Beloved One can be detected (v. 34–40). In the Báb's and Bahá'u'lláh's writings, the inmost reality of all Manifestations is the one divine reality of God's holy Spirit. In this sense, the Báb and Bahá'u'lláh are essentially one. Distinctions between them only exist from an historical point of view—distinctions such as physical ages, lineages, personalities, and specific writings. This unity and distinction is observable in a subtle ambiguity in the text.

The term *Youth* is referred to four times in the text, using two different terms in the original language. In the first instance, it is preceded by an adjective translated here as *Arabian* (*Iraqi* in the original). The Báb was a descendent of the Prophet Muḥammad, and as such he wore a green turban indicating this holy lineage. But in mystical literature, the "Arabian" youth is so archetypal that it is not clear that this description is intended to suggest anything about the Báb's linage or ancestry. The Maid of Heaven's reference to the "Arabian Youth" could be interpreted as a reference to the Báb, since the Báb used this terminology to refer to himself; or it could be assumed that, like the following references to the Youth, this refers to Bahá'u'lláh.[75] Certainly, the other references to the Youth are likely to be references to Bahá'u'lláh.[76] The text is ambiguous, since at that time a correlation between this terminology and the Báb was already known. But the text subtly suggests his oneness with the Báb, while alluding to what was then his own theophanic secret. In his later writings, Bahá'u'lláh indicates that he had a theophanic experience while imprisoned in the Síyáh-Chál in 1852. He later represented this event in his writings as a vision of a celestial Maid of Heaven, but he kept the significance of this experience a secret until April of 1863.[77] So, at the time he wrote the Tablet of the Holy Mariner, his mission was still concealed.

Bahá'u'lláh suggests this secret in two subtle ways. First, the Maid of Heaven states that the Youth is now *"hidden within the tabernacle of light by reason of that which the hands of the wicked have wrought"* (v. 36). To a certain degree this could be applicable to the Báb as his station is largely unrecognized, not only because of those who persecuted him and even ordered his execution, but also because the Bábí community had for a period suffered moral and spiritual decline. Nevertheless, the idea that the Youth is *"hidden"* could refer to Bahá'u'lláh's situation at the time the Tablet was composed, since it was owing to the actions of others that the disclosure of his mission was prevented from taking place. The second clue is less elusive. The handmaiden who searches the world for evidences of love for the Youth cries out, that *"the Youth hath remained lone and forlorn in the land of exile in the hands of the ungodly"* (v. 51). This tragic disclosure is the central message in the concluding portion of the Tablet. At the time the Tablet was revealed, it had been thirteen years since the Báb was executed in Tabriz, Persia. Although the words *"lone and forlorn in the land of exile"* could be applied to the Báb in a symbolic sense (that is, as an exile from people's hearts), this is a literal description of Bahá'u'lláh's situation in Baghdad.

When Bahá'u'lláh wrote the Tablet of the Holy Mariner he was 46 years old, which seems too old to be considered a youth. In order to understand Bahá'u'lláh's characterization of the Báb and himself as youths, it is helpful to appreciate the symbolic way in which this language is used in mystical poetry. Twice when referring to the quest for the Youth, references are made to the fragrance or perfume (v. 36) of the Youth's robe, or of the robes of those who associate with the Youth, who is also described as the Beloved One (v. 40). These descriptions, along with the idea of a lone exile reflect aspects of the story of Joseph, regarded as the best of stories in the Qur'an and a favorite point of reference in Islamic mystical literature. Joseph is an archetype, his youthful beauty being symbolic, signifying the beauty of God. He is for example equated with Ḥusayn in popular ta'ziyah performance.[78]

In the Book of Genesis, the youthful Joseph dreams that all will bow down in homage to him.[79] When his brothers hear about Joseph's dream they plot against him. Eventually they sell him into slavery, and he is taken into Egypt[80] where his true greatness is revealed. As in the case of Joseph, it was those who were closest to Bahá'u'lláh who were responsible for his bondage, most notably his half-brother, Mírzá Yaḥyá.[81] Joseph enters Egypt in bondage, but he proves his greatness by his devotion to God, by his prophecies, and by the many other signs he gives.[82] Eventually, his sovereignty is established. Similarly, Bahá'u'lláh is exiled to 'Akká, arriving in bondage. But through his greatness, his imprisonment is relaxed and his spiritual sovereignty is recognized.

It is also said that the young Joseph was incomparably beautiful and, because of this, Potiphar's wife Zulaykhá sought to seduce him. In mystical literature, this beauty of Joseph signifies the ancient and eternal beauty of God's holiness. Bahá'u'lláh, referring to all the Manifestations of God, frequently says, *"by their countenance the Beauty of God is revealed."*[83] Hence the title, "Ancient Beauty." The story of Joseph's beauty figures prominently in many Islamic mystical writings, and it is likely that the ideal Arabian Youth which also appears in Sufi mystical text is the reason Bahá'u'lláh uses it symbolically to refer to the Báb and to himself. Zulaykhá's attempts to seduce Joseph result eventually in his imprisonment. Out of love for Joseph's beauty, the lover brings harm to Joseph. Joseph is imprisoned for sins that were actually those of the misguided lover. This also has parallels to the ministry of Bahá'u'lláh, as he was imprisoned and suffered exile because a few misguided Bábís sought to assassinate the Shah of Persia as revenge for the execution of the Báb.[84] This act resulted in the imprisonment and execution of many Bábís.[85]

Because of his grief over the loss of his son, Jacob—Joseph's father—lost his sight.[86] But when the garment of Joseph was brought into his presence, Jacob recognized it immediately by its fragrance and the realization that Joseph was still alive restored Jacob's sight.[87] This symbolism comes into force early in Bahá'u'lláh's writings when, in a treatise written to the learned Shaykh 'Abdu'r-Rahmán known as The Four Valleys, Bahá'u'lláh alludes to the fragrance of his divinity:

> *Methinks at this moment, I catch the fragrance of His garment blowing from the Egypt of Bahá; verily He seemeth near at hand, though men may think Him far away. My soul doth smell the perfume shed by the Beloved One; My sense is filled with the fragrance of My dear Companion.*[88]

This type of symbolism reappears in the Tablet of the Holy Mariner when the maiden descends from heaven in hopes of inhaling the *"perfume of the robe from the Youth."* In the quranic version of the story of Joseph, the loss and restoration of Jacob's sight, like the death of the maiden in the Tablet of the Holy Mariner, may have many meanings. For example, without the presence of Joseph (i.e., the divine presence) there can be only grief in the world—the loss of spiritual vision, or in the case of the maiden, the loss of life itself (v. 53). The fragrance of Joseph's garment— signifying love of God and the divine teachings—is God's remedy that heals those who suffer in this world. The handmaiden entered this world searching for the fragrance of the Beloved. But when she could not find it, she died and ascended, returning to the higher worlds of God (v. 53). Also, when Joseph first told his father of his dream (i.e., proclaimed his mission), Jacob—who symbolizes the nation of Israel (hence, his name is also "Israel"[89])—did not realize Joseph's true significance. But the people of Israel were able to see the true greatness of his station when it was seen that he was alive in Egypt and had turned adversity into triumph and made his own unjust imprisonment a door of hope for both those among his own nation and those in Egypt.[90] His own people turned against him, hence, as with other Prophets, Joseph's greatness was first established among another people (signified by the Egyptians). Joseph not only provided a refuge in Egypt for the deliverance of his family, he received and forgave his oppressors.[91] This is what God had willed from the beginning. Realizing this, Jacob's sight was opened. Bahá'u'lláh writes:

> *O My Brother! Until thou enter the Egypt of love, thou shalt never come to the Joseph of the Beauty of the Friend; and until, like Jacob, thou forsake thine outward eyes, thou shalt never open the eye of thine inward being; and until thou burn with the fire of love, thou shalt never commune with the Lover of Longing.*[92]

The symbolism of Joseph's robe also has a parallel in the New Testament. This is seen in how people, whose faith is strong, are healed by touching merely the garment of Jesus.[93] All of these clues, the fragrance of the robe, the youthful Beloved, the exile into another land allude back to the story of Joseph to infuse the Tablet of the Holy Mariner with many layers of meaning including prophetic suggestions about the life ahead for Bahá'u'lláh. In a more personal and less historic sense, all people have within them the true Joseph which through their own actions has been exiled and is waiting to be discovered.

With the above introduction to the symbolism used in the Tablet of the Holy Mariner, it will now be easier to examine the text of the Tablet, section by section, in hopes of better understanding its overall message.

5

REFLECTIONS ON THE TABLET OF THE HOLY MARINER: A VERSE-BY-VERSE ANALYSIS

The following commentary assumes familiarity with the symbols explained in Chapter 4. These explanations do not exhaust the rich interpretive possibilities and meanings that can be extracted from the symbols in the Tablet, but they will provide a basic starting point for its understanding. The original stories and related symbols have in themselves been the source of countless commentaries and interpretations over the years, and, no doubt, will continue to be into the future.

As is characteristic of many of Bahá'u'lláh's Tablets, the Tablet of the Holy Mariner begins with an invocation, *"He is the Gracious, the Well-Beloved!"*[1] The text includes two refrains throughout that sustain this invocation: *"Glorified be my Lord, the All-Glorious!"* and *"Glorified be our Lord, the Most High!"*[2] This invocation and the following refrains are important to the Tablet as they help maintain the seeker's devotional orientation and add great aesthetic beauty and power to the recitation of the verses. For the purpose of the following analysis, however, the main verses of the Tablet will be examined together in separate sections without the refrains, in order to give greater clarity to the ideas that develop in the text.

Text

1 *O Holy Mariner! Bid thine ark of eternity appear before the Celestial Concourse,*

2 *Launch it upon the ancient sea, in His Name, the Most Wondrous,*
3 *And let the angelic spirits enter, in the Name of God, the Most High.*
4 *Unmoor it, then, that it may sail upon the ocean of glory,*
5 *Haply the dwellers therein may attain the retreats of nearness in the everlasting realm.*
6 *Having reached the sacred strand, the shore of the crimson seas,*
7 *Bid them issue forth and attain this ethereal invisible station,*
8 *A station wherein the Lord hath in the Flame of His Beauty appeared within the deathless tree;*
9 *Wherein the embodiments of His Cause cleansed themselves of self and passion;*
10 *Around which the Glory of Moses doth circle with the everlasting hosts;*
11 *Wherein the Hand of God was drawn forth from His bosom of Grandeur;*
12 *Wherein the ark of the Cause remaineth motionless even though to its dwellers be declared all divine attributes.*

Reflections on verses 1–12

In these opening verses the potential of seekers to journey to the higher worlds of God is presented. The Holy Mariner makes the ark appear (v. 1), launches it on the sea (v. 2), brings on board its passengers and sets sail (v. 3-4). The spiritual guide is the Mariner. This guide is essential for the journey. He delivers the ark to the passengers to board and it is at his command that it arrives at its destination. Otherwise, they have no ark of their own to carry them together and safely to their goal. All great mystics acknowledge the wisdom of seeking out such a master guide. Rúmí likens the Prophets and saints specifically to Noah's ark in several instances.[3]

> In the Sea of the Spirit, swimming is of no avail: Noah's ark is the
>   only escape.
> Muḥammad, that king of the prophets, said, "I am the ship in this
>   Universal Ocean,
> I, or that person who has become my true vicegerent in inward
>   vision."[4]

The greatest guides are luminaries such as Jesus, Muḥammad, Buddha, and Bahá'u'lláh. The great Muslim philosopher and mystic, Ibn 'Arabi points out,

"Although the two classes [prophets and saints] share a common ground—the stations of divine realization—still the ascent of the prophets is through the fundamental light itself, while the ascent of the saints is through what is providentially granted by that light."[5]

The ark's role develops in stages—appearance, boarding, transporting—each unfolding at the bidding of God and through the mediation of the Mariner. Similar, each stage signifies a corresponding stage in the journey of the seeker. The journey follows a route, a sacred geography, that appears to be modeled on the physical geography of the Middle East. But even more specifically, the sacred route recalls the Israelites wanderings in Sinai and their journey of liberation. The ark comes to the shore of *"the crimson seas"* (v. 6), and from this shore the passengers are taken to the deathless Tree—imagery suggesting the Sinai episode. Similarly, if a ship were travelling up the Red Sea, at the end of the Red Sea it would come to the *"the crimson seas"* at the southern tip of the Sinai peninsula where Mount Sinai is to be found. The plural *"crimson seas"* is likely to derive from the quranic verse, where Moses says he will not give up until he reaches the junction of the two seas or has spent years and years in travel. This junction of two seas referred to in the Qur'an is, as some have understood it to mean, the point where the two arms of the Red Sea come together, i.e., the meeting of the Gulf of 'Aqaba and the Gulf of Suez which enclose the Wilderness of Sinai.

The three references to bodies of water—the ancient sea, the ocean of glory, the crimson seas—though metaphorical, follow the course of a seafaring route from Persia to Sinai, from the Persian Gulf, to the Arabian Sea or Indian Ocean, to the Red Sea. The purpose here is not to advocate a literal reading of the Tablet, but rather to point out that it is likely that its metaphorical language is based on actual geography. The journey described, however, is an interior spiritual journey of the soul. But this use of the plural "seas," suggesting as it does Moses' determination and arduous journey mentioned in the Surah of the Cave (18:60), conveys something of the challenge of the spiritual life. Each of the terms used to describe the three bodies of water—*"ancient," "glory,"* and *"crimson"*—can be understood as references to the waters of revelation, representing its eternal, luminous, and redemptive nature. Every seeker comes to understand these seas according to individual effort, capacity, and experience, but all must pass over them to reach the sacred strand. The Tablet's message conveys God's desire to guide us to the heights of spirituality so that we can ultimately attain the center of heavenly guidance. The use of the Exodus symbolism is a way of re-affirming that the spiritual path remains a path of liberation—this is not a new teaching, but one that involves an ancient covenant and is a continuation of redemptive acts seen throughout time.⁶

But there is another important reason to understand this geographical symbolism. It is an evidence of the important prophetic nature of the Tablet. Just as the Tablet reveals archetypal symbols foretelling the opposition to Bahá'u'lláh and God's covenant that would occur in the future, so too the geographical symbolism represents parallel events in the history of Bahá'u'lláh's life just as it was about to unfold. A comparison of the basic geography in the Tablet with the exile route of Bahá'u'lláh shows that both traverse three main bodies of water and terminate at the base of holy mountains. In the Tablet, the ark appears to traverse the Persian Gulf, the Indian Ocean, and the Red Sea to arrive at Mount Sinai. Following the revelation of the Tablet of the Holy Mariner, Bahá'u'lláh traversed a route beginning at Baghdad that would likewise cross three major bodies of water: the Black Sea, the Aegean Sea, and the Mediterranean Sea. This route terminates on the shores of Palestine at the base of Mount Carmel.

The first stage of this seafaring prophecy is probably the basis for Shoghi Effendi's statement that "seven days after His arrival, He, as foreshadowed in the Tablet of the Holy Mariner, was put on board a Turkish steamer and three days later was disembarked, at noon, together with His fellow-exiles, at the port of

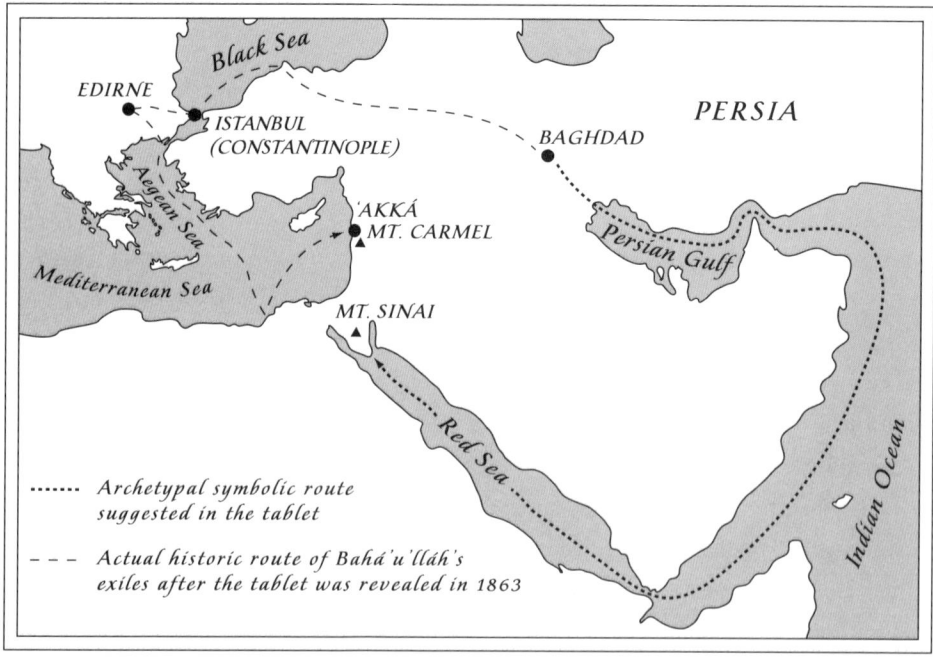

Constantinople, on the first of Rabí'u'l-Avval 1280 A.H. (August 16, 1863)."⁷ Just as the mystical ark of eternity traverses the seas in a journey to the Mountain of God, so too Bahá'u'lláh would literally traverse seas to arrive at Mount Carmel.

In the Tablet, the ark arrives at the shores of the crimson seas and the Mariner bids the passengers to leave the ark and attain a station which is a prelude to their ascent to heaven (v. 7). This station is the station wherein the beauty of the Lord is apparent (v. 8) and the passengers or seekers clean themselves of self and passion (v. 9).⁸ In this station the sovereignty of God is made apparent (v. 11), and all the divine attributes are declared. In these verses the first steps in the mystic ascent to the center of heavenly guidance are set forth, namely, purification and the disclosure of the knowledge of God.

Text

13 *O Mariner! Teach them that are within the ark that which we have taught thee behind the mystic veil,*

14 *Perchance they may not tarry in the sacred snow-white spot,*

15 *But may soar upon the wings of the spirit unto that station which the Lord hath exalted above all mention in the worlds below,*

16 *May wing through space even as the favored birds in the realm of eternal reunion;*

17 *May know the mysteries hidden in the Seas of light.*

18 *They passed the grades of worldly limitations and reached that of the divine unity, the center of heavenly guidance.*

Reflections on verses 13–18

It is understood commonly in mysticism, that the mystical path to God follows basic stages that most succinctly can be described as purification, knowledge, and union. From Mount Sinai, the Mariner is instructed to teach the passengers what he has been taught *"behind the mystic veil"* so that they may then ascend to heaven. The mystic veil is a symbol that has several recognizable antecedents.⁹ In Judaism, the Mosaic Tablets of the law were placed in an ark or box and placed in the tabernacle. The outer court of the tabernacle was separated by a veil and the ark containing the law, known as the Ark of the Covenant, was placed behind the veil. Only the high priest was permitted to go behind this veil and enter the presence of the Ark. In Sufi poetry, God is likened to a bride or maiden whose beauty is concealed by a veil. The lifting of the veil represents the disclosure of the divine. As in the marriage ceremony, only the bridegroom, the true lover of the bride is allowed to lift the veil. In the Tablet of the Holy Mariner, disclosing what was taught behind the mystic veil, is to disclose the hidden beauty of God to the true seekers.

This hidden knowledge of God disclosed by the Manifestations of God is, according to the terminology of scripture, expressed most succinctly in the *name of God*.[10] The name of God is itself symbolic according to Bahá'u'lláh's writings. In each age, the name of God is the Most Great Name, a name signified by the name of the Manifestation of God. At one time that name is Moses, at another Jesus, at another Muḥammad, and so on.[12] This knowledge is only apparent to those who perceive the one Spirit of God in all these Manifestations. This is the knowledge that reconciles religions and liberates the seeker from sectarianism and religious prejudices. In this age, Bahá'ís, for example, understand the hidden name of God to be represented by Bahá'u'lláh's teachings and signified by his name, *Bahá'u'lláh* (Arabic for *Glory of God*). The *name* signifies the presence of God. Truly knowing the name means having access to that divine presence, an access possible through knowledge of the teachings of God's Manifestations. In Bahá'í teaching, the Most Great Name of God is composed of the letters "B" and "H" from "Bahá" and includes derivations, such as *Alláh-u Abhá* (God the All-Glorious), and *Ya Bahá'u'l-Abhá* (O Thou Glory of Glories). In one of Bahá'u'lláh's last great works, he urges a notorious Muslim cleric who persecuted the Bahá'ís to renounce his evil ways and enter the crimson Ark. He then writes,

> *Shouldest thou enter therein and attain unto it, set thy face towards the Kaaba of God, the Help in Peril, the Self-Subsisting, and say: "O my God! I beseech Thee by Thy most glorious light, and all Thy lights are verily glorious." Thereupon, will the doors of the Kingdom be flung wide before thy face, and thou wilt behold what eyes have never beheld, and hear what ears have never heard.*[11]

The phrase, which looks outwardly like a magical formula, uses the word *glorious* twice, a term derived from the same root as the Most Great Name. The passage parallels the allegory in the first act of the Tablet of the Holy Mariner as if it were a commentary on it. The object of the verse—"*I beseech Thee by Thy most glorious light, and all Thy lights are verily glorious*"—is that the cleric should stop persecuting innocent people and recognize the light for what it is, and in whomever it has appeared. This recognition will enable him to enter the kingdom

Verse-by-Verse Analysis

of God where he will learn those transcendental truths that are above the visual and audible plain of existence.

The hidden knowledge that lies behind the mystic veil is a key that enables the seekers to ascend above the station wherein they first beheld the beauty of God in the valley of *ṭuwā*, signifying the outward forms of God's Manifestation in the created world. That is, this is the highest Manifestation of God in the world of creation. From this point they are encouraged to attain to a station which the *"Lord hath exalted above all mention in the worlds below"* (v. 15). This is the station wherein they ascend to God even as those who already inhabit the *"realm of eternal reunion"* (v. 16). This is the ultimate goal of the mystic and has been described by some as the beatific vision. In this station they know the mysteries hidden in *"the Seas of light"* (v. 17). This is a metaphor based on the constellations of stars in the nighttime sky. These stars signify the spiritual luminaries in the different religions, the great prophets, mystics, learned sages, and saints. This is the station wherein the seeker comes to know what these great holy persons know. Bahá'u'lláh writes:

> *If thou be a man of communion and prayer, soar up on the wings of assistance from Holy Souls, that thou mayest behold the mysteries of the Friend and attain to the lights of the Beloved.*[12]

In this stage, the seeker overcomes worldly limitations, those desires for prosperity and material gain that often lead people to forego spiritual virtues. In this realm, the seeker has reached the sphere of the *"divine unity"* which is *"the center of heavenly guidance."* In the context of the collective unity of the dwellers in the ark, this divine unity is also the condition of liberation from sectarianism through their collective recognition of the center of heavenly guidance—the spiritual guide.[13] In the broader context of mystical understanding, it is the divine unity that transcends the knowledge of the names and outward forms of ritual and dogma. In this condition the seeker sees the absolute unity of the different Manifestations, regardless of where or when or to whom they have appeared. *"In this station he pierceth the veils of plurality, fleeth from the worlds of the flesh, and ascendeth into the heaven of singleness."*[14]

Text

19 *They have desired to ascend unto that state which the Lord hath ordained to be above their stations.*

20 *Whereupon the burning meteor cast them out from them that abide in the Kingdom of His Presence,*

21 *And they heard the Voice of Grandeur raised from behind the unseen pavilion upon the Height of Glory:*

22 *"O guardian angels! Return them to their abode in the world below,*

23 *"Inasmuch as they have purposed to rise to that sphere which the wings of the celestial dove have never attained;*

24 *"Whereupon the ship of fancy standeth still which the minds of them that comprehend cannot grasp."*

Reflections on verses 19–24

In verse 19, it is clear that some of the angelic spirits have sought to transgress the limitations of their station. Because of this they are excluded from the presence of God and the company of the other angelic spirits (v. 20). These passages suggest many possible meanings, but to be concise, the symbolism suggests that pride, jealousy, envy, ambition for leadership, the willingness to harm others in the pursuit of power and prestige—these and other perennial weaknesses—are likely to be the source of alienation described in this allegory. Even as purification and sanctification are conducive to communion with God, corrupt inclinations lead to alienation.

At this stage of the allegory, the *"Voice of Grandeur"* states why these select angels are cast out—*"they have purposed to rise to that sphere which the wings of the celestial dove have never attained"* (v. 23). The Voice of Grandeur signifies God's voice, but in the world of existence, it could well be the voice of the Manifestations of God, since voice implies a mouth and thus an incarnate form that God does not possess. Or, keeping with the symbolism and following upon Jewish lore, the Voice of Grandeur could well be mediated by an angel.[15] In any event, the message suggests that there is a divine order that exists and that these angels are therefore cast out on account of the incompatibility of their desires with that order.

The last two verses in the Voice of Granduer's monologue (v. 23–24), especially verse 24, are elusive particularly in relation to the preceding verses. But one meaning appears to be as follows: The angels purposed to rise to that sphere which the wings of the celestial dove (referring to other angels) have never attained; a sphere at which point the ship of fancy (i.e., pride, vanity, and/or unattainable aspirations) is stopped and can go no further, having reached a point where even the minds of them that comprehend can grasp no more. In other words, these two verses stress three points

(1) no human, no matter how celestial, has ever reached the habitation of God, (2) all means (ships) and methods that might be imagined, fall short, are stopped, and are prevented from achieving this sphere of God, and (3) it is a station which even the most enlightened minds cannot grasp. Bahá'u'lláh writes:

> *Every mystic knower hath wandered far astray in the valley of the knowledge of Him; every saint hath lost his way in seeking to comprehend His Essence. Sanctified is He above the understanding of the wise; exalted is He above the knowledge of the knowing!*[16]

The presence of God is unattainable except through attaining the presence of God's Manifestations, persons such as Moses, Buddha, Christ, and Bahá'u'lláh. And such persons appear, as ordained by God, only rarely in history. It is through following their examples and teachings that people come to know God and attain His presence. They exemplify the path to God. As the great mystic Ibn 'Arabi writes: "And know that every saint of God Most High receives what he receives through the spiritual mediation of the prophet whose sacred Way he follows."[17]

Text

25 *Whereupon the maid of heaven looked out from her exalted chamber,*
26 *And with her brow signed to the Celestial Concourse,*
27 *Flooding with the light of her countenance the heaven and the earth,*
28 *And as the radiance of her beauty shone upon the people of dust,*
29 *All beings were shaken in their mortal graves.*
30 *She then raised the call which no ear through all eternity hath ever heard,*
31 *And thus proclaimed: "By the Lord! He whose heart hath not the fragrance of the love of the exalted and glorious Arabian Youth,*
32 *"Can in no wise ascend unto the glory of the highest heaven."*

Reflections on verses 25–32

In the opening verses of the Tablet, the Mariner calls the people into the ark of eternity and leads them beyond the shore of the crimson seas to teach them what will enable them to ascend to the center of heavenly guidance. This journey culminates with the angels being cast out of heaven for desiring what is not attainable for them, a station that is contrary to their nature. Now this message is reiterated in a different way. Instead of the Mariner gathering the angelic spirits together, the Maid of Heaven will take up a mission of search for faithful souls. In one sense this search could refer to a second chance for those *"claimants"* who were cast out. In a second sense, it could refer to others among the religious community still on earth searching for the expected Beloved or making similar claims to the first group who were cast out of heaven. In a third and more hyperbolic sense, the text can be read to mean that those in the religious community have failed and been cast out, now the search turns toward those outside the community.

After the fall of the angels, the Maid of Heaven appears (v. 25). She is a luminous beings, who according to the biblical tradition appears whenever a prophet or friend of God is in need. This suggests that the fall of the angels somehow represents an hour of distress for the friends of God on earth. With her *"brow,"* a poetic way of expressing a person's rational faculty, she illumines both heaven and earth. This revelation of beatific light shakes all beings in their mortal graves: It is through the revelation of immortality that mortality is revealed, the light of truth causes the shadows of falsehood to be cast; the disclosure of righteousness makes known the weaknesses of our characters. In this way, the Maiden is the touchstone of truth. Her light and beauty make both truth and error known. This touchstone of truth is expressed in the Maiden's pronouncement that *"he whose heart hath not the fragrance of the love of the exalted and glorious Arabian Youth, can in no wise ascend unto the glory of the highest heaven"* (v. 31–32). Since the text is intentionally elusive, it can be read in many different ways. In one sense it can be interpreted as a further expression of why the angels were cast out; that is, had they loved the Beloved they would not have sought to usurp his station. In another sense, the statement is a criterion or touchstone for every seeker. That is, one should know this truth so that one does not follow another path that does not lead to the highest heaven, such as any path a fallen angel who now inhabits the community might propose.

The *"Arabian Youth"* (v. 31) was known among the Bábís to be a reference to the Báb. But in its inmost significance it symbolizes the Spirit of God which the seeker should recognize wherever it appears.

The assertion that the Maiden's call was a message that no *"ear through all eternity hath ever heard"* (v. 30) is enigmatic. In one sense, it appears to be hyperbole intended to heighten the sense of spiritual pathos one feels from witnessing waywardness in the religious community. That is, no ear has heard it because no ear was found willing to listen to it. Otherwise, it is a call that has always been raised throughout all of created existence. More literally, it could be interpreted to refer to the Báb in particular, that is, that this is a new call to faith, a call to recognize and follow the Báb.

Text

33 Thereupon she summoned unto herself one maiden from her handmaidens,
34 And commanded her: "Descend into space from the mansions of eternity,
35 "And turn thou unto that which they have concealed in the inmost of their hearts.
36 "Shouldst thou inhale the perfume of the robe from the Youth that hath been hidden within the tabernacle of light by reason of that which the hands of the wicked have wrought,
37 "Raise a cry within thyself, that all the inmates of the chambers of Paradise, that are the embodiments of the eternal wealth, may understand and hearken;
38 "That they may all come down from their everlasting chambers and tremble,
39 "And kiss their hands and feet for having soared to the heights of faithfulness;
40 "Perchance they may find from their robes the fragrance of the Beloved One."

Reflections on verses 33–40

This following scenario recalls Wisdom (Sophia) in the Book of Proverbs sending her handmaidens out to invite the faithful to a heavenly banquet. Having made her pronouncement, the Maiden now calls upon one of her handmaidens and entrusts her with a mission (v. 33–34). The object of the mission is to find those among the dwellers of the earth who show signs of love for the Beloved One (v. 35–36). The purpose of this quest is to find these souls so that the inmates of heaven can pay homage to them (v. 38–40).

The Beloved One is described as *"the Youth"* who is hidden in the tabernacle of light because of what the wicked have done (v. 36). In this instance the earlier narrative may be overlapping, that is, the wicked may well be a reference to the fallen angels. More likely, in the historical context it includes those who attempted to assassinate the Shah of Persia in revenge for the execution of the

Báb, an act that was responsible for Bahá'u'lláh's exile. More symbolically, it is the wickedness within all people that causes the Beloved to be exiled from their hearts. The Beloved is not hiding from them, rather their actions cause the Beloved to be hidden from their sight.

The handmaiden's mission, reflecting the classical love poetry of the mystics, testifies to the ardent desire of true seekers to find any trace of the object of their quest. The inmates of heaven are willing to come down from heaven to kiss the hands and feet of the faithful, not just to reward them, but for the chance they may find from their robes the fragrance of the Beloved One. Since this fragrance of the Beloved represents the love of God, and since the steed of this path of love is pain,[18] the heavenly concourse wishes to show its admiration for the seekers.

Text

41 *Thereupon the countenance of the favored damsel beamed above the celestial chambers even as the light that shineth from the face of the Youth above His mortal temple;*

42 *She then descended with such an adorning as to illumine the heavens and all that is therein.*

43 *She bestirred herself and perfumed all things in the lands of holiness and grandeur.*

44 *When she reached that place she rose to her full height in the midmost heart of creation,*

45 *And sought to inhale their fragrance at a time that knoweth neither beginning nor end.*

46 *She found not in them that which she did desire, and this, verily, is but one of His wondrous tales.*

47 *She then cried aloud, wailed and repaired to her own station within her most lofty mansion,*

48 *And then gave utterance to one mystic word, whispered privily by her honeyed tongue,*

49 *And raised the call amidst the Celestial Concourse and the immortal maids of heaven:*

50 *"By the Lord! I found not from these idle claimants the breeze of Faithfulness!*

51 *"By the Lord! The Youth hath remained lone and forlorn in the land of exile in the hands of the ungodly."*

Verse-by-Verse Analysis

Reflections on verses 41–51

Following the Maiden's instructions, the favored handmaiden is radiant with happiness for having this opportunity (v. 41). She adorns and perfumes herself befittingly for this great occasion (v. 42, 43). Her perfume and adornments signify her pure motive to serve humankind and her attitude of devotion. When she reaches the spot which is the inmost heart of the people of this world (v. 44), she seeks to discover signs of love for the Beloved (v. 45). The fact that she is unable to find any trace of the Beloved at *"a time that knoweth neither beginning nor end"* (v. 45) appears to be a hyperbolic expression, that is, an assertion that people neither in the past nor in the future show any sign of love for the Beloved. This distressing realization crushes her spirit and she wails with grief and returns to her dwelling place in heaven.

She then whispers one mystic word. At this point the text is again elusive. What is the mystic word? Is it the call that she raises among the Celestial Concourse or is it some other secret? Bahá'u'lláh writes, *"Volumes will not suffice to hold the mystery of the Beloved One . . . although it be no more than a word, no more than a sign."*[19]

The call she raises among the Celestial Concourse and the immortal maids of heaven is her solemn twofold testimony that she found no one who was truly faithful and that the Beloved remained alone and forlorn *"in the land of exile in the hands of the ungodly."* Those that she accuses of faithlessness are referred to as *"idle claimants,"* a description that could refer to those who during the years after the Báb's martyrdom would claim falsely to be his successor or the revealer of God's light. Or more broadly, it could refer to anyone who claims to be the follower of a religion or religious path but who is actually unfaithful to the spiritual life.

Text

52 *She then uttered within herself such a cry that the Celestial Concourse did shriek and tremble,*

53 *And she fell upon the dust and gave up the spirit. It seemeth she was called and hearkened unto Him that summoned her unto the Realm on High.*

54 *Glorified be He that created her out of the essence of love in the midmost heart of his exalted paradise!*

55 *Thereupon the maids of heaven hastened forth from their chambers, upon whose countenances the eye of no dweller in the highest paradise had ever gazed.*

56 *They all gathered around her, and lo! they found her body fallen upon the dust;*

57 *And as they beheld her state and comprehended a word of the tale told by the Youth, they bared their heads, rent their garments asunder, beat upon their faces, forgot their joy, shed tears and smote with their hands upon their cheeks, and this is verily one of the mysterious grievous afflictions—*

Reflections on verses 52–57

These last verses present us with the image of the dead handmaiden. She has entered the world of existence, her quest has ended in failure, and she has then died of grief. Her spirit is then resurrected to the Realm on High. The maids of heaven come forth and grieve over her death.

Since the Tablet of the Holy Mariner is an allegorical tale, it is helpful to consider how Bahá'u'lláh has constructed the story and used symbols to reflect his own views on spirituality. In his earlier work, the Book of Certitude, Bahá'u'lláh explains at length the meaning of true spiritual sovereignty.[20] He, for example, explains that although to outward appearances the martyrdom of the Imám Ḥusayn was a tragedy, inwardly it was also a great spiritual victory. Ḥusayn's willing sacrifice demonstrated his true spiritual station. In the same way, he explains that outwardly, Jesus appeared to be poor, but spiritually he was rich.[21] The aim of these explanations is to encourage the seeker to look deeper and appreciate the intrinsic value of the spiritual life. It is commentary on the age-old question of why God allows the just to suffer and the unjust to prosper.

These teachings have significance for the interpretation of the Tablet of the Holy Mariner. There are, for example, several features in the symbolism at the end of the Tablet that suggest a positive, rather than a tragic message. In the allegory, the handmaiden dies from grief when she is unable to find a trace of the fragrance of the Beloved. However, this grief should not be separated from its cause, which is the condition of humanity. The end of the Tablet is focused on the problems of: corruption in the world, the disillusionment and grief that comes from witnessing strife among members of a religious community, and the experience of betrayal by companion seekers.

A great sense of personal well-being, harmony, and growth can be obtained from companionship with like-minded seekers or participation in a religious community that combines its energies for the benefit of humanity. Nevertheless, such associations and friendships can also be a severe test of faith and a profound source of grief when jealousy and betrayal occur, or corruption is discovered. Hence, the often heard criticism of organized religion. When a person is involved in a religious community that person is most vulnerable, since in those circumstances one is least likely to suspect the selfish intentions of others. This factor will always make religious groups a haven for people who want to take advantage of others for personal gain. The worst of the fallen angels are not stereotypical criminals or recognizable devils with horns, but rather persons who have sailed in the ark through the waters of God's revelation and begun the ascent to heaven. Such people are able to command the admiration and trust of unsuspecting seekers. Bahá'u'lláh's Tablet of the Holy Mariner anticipates this occurrence and aims to prepare and reassure seekers when they find themselves having to cope with this perennial problem. This lesson can be taken from several features of the allegory.

The handmaiden at the end of the Tablet already belongs to a higher spiritual realm, yet when she searches the world and finds only corruption, she dies of grief. She passes yet again into another higher realm, drawing even closer to God. The message here is that when a seeker's eyes are opened to corruption within the community, no matter how disillusioning this experience may be, through it God can enable the seeker to attain to a new level of spiritual awareness and communion. In this instance, its a level of faith freed and liberated from dependence on the faith and conduct of others.

When the handmaiden dies, other maids of heaven hastened forth from their chambers, upon whose countenances Bahá'u'lláh says *"the eye of no dweller in the highest paradise had ever gazed."* This phrase is rich with meaning. The Qur'an uses the symbolism of maidens when describing the rewards of the faithful in the hereafter. They are *"virgin-pure (and undefiled)"* whom *"no man or Jinn before them has touched," "fair (companions), good and beautiful."*[22] In Bahá'u'lláh's Book of Certitude, this symbolism of the unseen and untouched maids of heaven (Arabic, húrís) is given a more explicit religious meaning. The virginity of the quranic maidens is interpreted as a symbol for untouched or undiscovered spiritual insights.[23] This symbolism suggests that there is a message of hope underlying the tragic ending of the Tablet of the Holy Mariner. That is, through the death of the handmaiden, other hidden meanings come forth and are disclosed. However painful it may be, such experiences create new possibilities for greater understanding and deeper faith. The handmaiden has resurrected to a higher level in heaven, signifying higher attainments in that world, while in this world the new hidden meanings have also appeared. Even moments of deepest despair and grief can be a door to greater insight and spiritual consciousness.

Notes

PREFACE

1. Jan Rypka, *History of Iranian Literature*, p. 109.

CHAPTER 1: THE AUTHORSHIP AND DATE OF THE TABLET

1. One of the earliest primary sources of historical information considered authoritative among Bahá'ís is a historical narrative written by Muhammad-i Zarandí (1831–1892), who is known as Nabíl-i-A'zam. A portion of this narrative was edited and translated by Shoghi Effendi and published in 1932 under the title *The Dawn-Breakers: Nabíl's Narrative of the Early Days of the Bahá'í Revelation*. This work, composed in the 1880s, is a heroic gospel-like epic written from a believer's point of view with the aim of inspiring faith in the supernatural character of events and persons involved in the birth of this great spiritual episode in human history. The portion translated into English covers a period from the late ministry of Shaykh Ahmad-i Ahsá'í (1753–1834) up to the time of Bahá'u'lláh's exile from Persia in 1852. This work contains few historical details from the early life of Bahá'u'lláh, but it does mention Bahá'u'lláh's reputation as a great sage and beneficent man in his native region prior to his recognition of the Báb's religious claims. See Nabíl-i A'zam, *The Dawn-Breakers*, p. 106.
2. This mulla was the first disciple of the Báb, a man by the name of Mullá Husayn from the town of Bárfurúsh. For twelve years (1831–44) Mullá Husayn-i Bárfurúsh had been an adherent of the Shaykhí movement and follower of Sayyid Kazim, the successor of Shaykh Ahmad. According to the Bahá'í historian Nabíl-i A'zam, Mullá Husayn was thirty-six years old when he was martyred in 1848, in a siege lead by government forces opposed to the Bábí movement. See Nabíl-i A'zam, *The Dawn-Breakers*, p. 383.
3. The Báb's writings are infused with an apocalyptic tone suggesting the immanent appearance of the Day of Judgment (see The Báb, *Selections*, pp. 41, 43, 44, 53, 61, 63). His more expository works taught that the anticipated Day of Judgment had already arrived and that outwardly that Day was like any other day (see The Báb,

Selections, pp. 78–9). While this interpretation reflects a realized eschatology, it is not clear how well these teachings were understood among early adherents. The contents of Bahá'u'lláh's Book of Certitude, written in 1862, indicate that these issues still needed clarification.

4. The anticipation of a great spiritual figure dominates much of the Báb's writings. The Báb often speaks of this person as "Him Whom God shall make manifest" (*man yuẓhiruhu'lláh*). See, for example, the Báb, *Selections*, pp. 83, 85, 86, 89, 95, 130–6.

5. In 1897 the Board of Foreign Missions of the Presbyterian Church of the United States writes with regard to the situation in Persia: "During the last thirty years the whole body of Moslems has been convulsed by the new religion of the Báb." (Board of Foreign Missions of the Presbyterian Church U.S.A., *Historical Sketches of the Missions*, p. 242). In 1899 one observer recounted, in a history of the Church Missionary Society, that the Bábís were "a remarkable sect which, in the past half-century, has spread in Persia with extraordinary rapidity. The whole story of this strange and in many respects hopeful religious movement is of extreme interest. Thousands of Bábís were cruelly put to death in the late shah's reign, and others fiercely persecuted; 'but the more they afflicted them the more they multiplied and grew'" (Eugene Stock, *The History of the Church Missionary Society*, vol. 3, p. 753). The same publication acknowledges that the "Bábís" hold the Bible "in great reverence" and are "most friendly to Christians" whom they regard as "brethren."

6. The Báb directed his disciples, whom he called "Letters of the Living," to return to their native regions to spread his teachings. One of his disciples was Shaykh Sa'íd-i Hindí, the ninth Letter of the Living, whom he directed to return to India. A few years later, the Báb was sought out by a dervish, whom the Báb named Qahru'lláh and whom he also directed to return to India to spread his teachings. See Nabíl-i A'ẓam, *The Dawn-Breakers*, pp. 305–306, 588.

7. See Nabíl-i A'ẓam, *The Dawn-Breakers*, pp. 112–18.

8. The Báb wrote, "The path to guidance is one of love and compassion, not of force and coercion. This hath been God's method in the past, and shall continue to be in the future! He causeth him whom He pleaseth to enter the shadow of His Mercy. Verily, He is the Supreme Protector, the All-Generous." (The Báb, *Selections*, p. 77).

9. Many years later, while recounting the early experience of imprisonment in Tehran, Bahá'u'lláh wrote: "God knows what We endured in that gloomy and loathsome place! By day and by night, in this prison We reflected on the condition of the Bábís and their doings and affairs, wondering how, notwithstanding their greatness of soul, nobility, and intelligence, they could be capable of such a deed as this audacious attempt on the life of the sovereign. Then did this wronged One determine that, on leaving this prison, He would arise with the utmost endeavour for the regeneration of these souls." See Nabíl-i A'ẓam, *The Dawn-Breakers*, p. 609. See also Bahá'u'lláh, *Epistle*, p. 21.

10. As many as twenty-five persons had advanced the claim to be the leader of the Bábí community. See H. M. Balyuzi's biographical account of the life of Bahá'u'lláh, *Bahá'u'lláh: The King of Glory*, p. 121.

11. Bahá'u'lláh, *Certitude*, p. 251

12. For a brief survey of this period see Juan Ricardo Cole, "Bahá'u'lláh and the Naqshbandí Sufis in Iraq," *From Iran East and West: Studies in Bábí and Bahá'í History*, vol. 4, pp. 1–28.

Notes

13. The Haft Vádí (the Seven Valleys) is a mystical essay written by Bahá'u'lláh to a knowledgeable Shaykh, Muhyi'd-Dín. The essay follows the structure of Farídu'd-Dín 'Attár's seven valleys found in his poetic masterpiece, *The Conference of the Birds*. Internal evidence suggests that Bahá'u'lláh's intention was largely to validate the mystical teachings commonly associated with the path to God while steering the seeker away from monistic doctrinal tendencies. One of the text's most intriguing sections is Bahá'u'lláh's interpretation of the individual letters composing the Persian word for a common sparrow.
14. Nabíl-i A'zam (1831–1892) was posthumously designated as one of the Apostles of Bahá'u'lláh by Shoghi Effendi. According to his own testimony, he was only sixteen years old when he overheard a conversation which first made him aware of the Báb's teachings. See Nabíl-i A'zam, *The Dawn-Breakers*, pp. 434–5. Upon Bahá'u'lláh's death, Nabíl was so grief stricken that he drowned himself in the Mediterranean. See H. M. Balyuzi, *Eminent Bahá'ís in the Time of Bahá'u'lláh*, pp. 268–9.
15. In a letter dated 31 July 1997, the Bahá'í World Centre Research Department conveyed to this writer that the Bahá'í Archives contains an incomplete copy of the Tablet of the Holy Mariner that is identified as being in the actual handwriting of Bahá'u'lláh. They also possess seven other copies of the Arabic section of the Tablet in other scripts. Because the copy in Bahá'u'lláh's handwriting is incomplete, a copy in the handwriting of 'Abdu'l-Bahá is designated the primary copy. It has the inscription "152" in Bahá'u'lláh's handwriting and is catalogued at the Bahá'í World Centre under the number BC001/001/01037. At this time no precise determination of the date of the earliest manuscript has been made. With regard to the earliest publications, they further explained that many of the Tablets of Bahá'u'lláh "were not 'published' in the currently accepted sense of the word," but were reproduced and widely distributed in the East by making "a 'master' in the hand of a respected calligrapher and then reproducing this copy by means of a gelatin-based copying devise. . . . This method of 'publication' is known to be the case in the instance of the Tablet of the Holy Mariner."

    In the broad context of Bahá'u'lláh's writings, the Tablet of the Holy Mariner belongs to the early period in both date and content. Prior to 1863, Bahá'u'lláh's most important and well-known writings—such as the Book of Certitude, the Hidden Words, the Seven Valleys, the Four Valleys—focus on the individual's search, the necessary spiritual and ethical discipline required for that search, and instruction in how to understand certain central spiritual truths. In the Seven Valleys and Four Valleys, Bahá'u'lláh, for example, discusses the stages in the search to attain the presence of God. The Hidden Words focuses on the necessary ethical prerequisites for the seeker's quest, and the Book of Certitude clarifies various doctrinal and interpretive problems that often perplex people seeking to understand the meaning and significance of the spiritual life. After 1863, Bahá'u'lláh most well-known writings—his Tablets to various monarchs and religious leaders, the Kitáb-i Aqdas, Bishárát, Tajallíyát, Tarázát, and others—continue many of these themes but with an expanding emphasis on the well being of the community of believers and the world as a whole. These writings contain teachings concerning the oneness of humankind, religious toleration, and various teachings aimed at bringing about collective security for all humankind—teachings concerning the need for disarmament, establishing a universal language, eliminating the extremes of wealth and poverty.
16. The actual nature of Bahá'u'lláh's declaration of his religious mission is hard to ascertain. Shoghi Effendi, who was the appointed successor of 'Abdu'l-Bahá, Bahá'u'lláh's son,

wrote: "The words Bahá'u'lláh actually uttered on that occasion, the manner of His Declaration, the reaction it produced, its impact on Mírzá Yahyá, the identity of those who were privileged to hear Him, are shrouded in an obscurity which future historians will find it difficult to penetrate" (Shoghi Effendi, *God Passes By* 153). How and to what extent he indicated that he was the one anticipated by the Báb is unclear. It is only in later writings that documentary evidence can be found for the study of his religious claims. Several scholars have, however, attempted to clarify the nature of Bahá'u'lláh's early disclosure. See Juan Cole's "Bahá'u'lláh's 'Súrah of the Companions': An Early Edirne Tablet of Declaration (c. 1864)" in *Bahā'ī Studies Bulletin*, pp. 4–30 (vol. 5:3, June 1991) and Stephen Lambden's "Some Notes on Bahá'u'lláh's Gradually Evolving Claims of the Adrianople/Edirne Period" pp. 75–83, in *Bahā'ī Studies Bulletin*, pp. 4–30 (vol. 5:3, June 1991).

CHAPTER 2: THE LITERARY STYLE OF THE TABLET
1. The Persian text contains maxims and exhortations and is less allegorical.
2. Bahá'u'lláh wrote in different styles and referred to different works as tablets, súrihs, books, prayers, epistles, and odes. The Arabic terms *súrih* and *lawh* are often translated into English as "Tablet." The word *súrih* is a term used to refer to divisions of the Qur'an. The term *lawh* is the same term used in the Qur'an and Arabic Bible when referring to the Tablets of Moses brought down from Mount Sinai (see for example, Qur'an 7:145, 150, 154; Exodus 24:12, 31:18). Both terms appear to have been used by Bahá'u'lláh to indicate the spiritual sanctity of the text.
3. Shoghi Effendi's translation of the Tablet of the Holy Mariner can be found in a number of recent publications, such as *Bahá'í Prayers* published by the Bahá'í Publishing Trust of the United States and the Bahá'í Publishing Trust of the United Kingdom, in *Writings of Bahá'u'lláh*, published by the Bahá'í Publishing Trust of India (1986) and in *Bahá'í Prayers for Women* and *Prayers of Ecstasy* published by Kalimat Press (2001). In addition to the early Bahá'í periodical, *Star of the West* (May 1922 edition), it appeared in a 1923 compilation titled *Baha'i Scriptures: Selections from the Utterances of Baha'u'llah and Abdul Baha* using very different capitalizations throughout. Shoghi Effendi's translation of the Tablet of the Holy Mariner also has special spiritual status among Bahá'ís because he was the appointed interpreter of Bahá'u'lláh's writings. According to information supplied by the Bahá'í World Centre Research Department, editions in Arabic include *Má'idiy-yi Ásimání* (Tehrán: Bahá'í Publishing Trust, 104 B.E.), vol. 2, pp. 507–14, republished in a reorganized edition of *Má'idiy-yi Ásimání* twenty-five years later (129 B.E.), vol. 4, pp. 335–341 and an elegant calligraphic version published by Bahá'í-Verlag in Langenhain, Germany in 1985.
4. A series of interesting articles explaining the origins and characteristics of *ta'ziyah* are available in *Ta'zieh: Ritual and Drama in Iran*, edited by Peter J. Chelkowski (1979). A two volume nineteenth-century transcript from oral traditions depicting various scenes of such performances was published by Sir Lewis Pelly. See Pelly, *The Miracle Play of Hasan and Husain: Collected from oral tradition*, volumes I and II (1879).
5. Shí'ah Islam, a large sect among Muslims, and the predominant religion of Iran, holds that 'Alí, the husband of Fátimih, the Prophet Muhammad's daughter, was the appointed and rightful successor of Muhammad and therefore, the spiritual Guide (Imám) of the community. Following 'Alí's assassination, they hold that 'Alí's two sons,

Notes

Ḥasan and Ḥusayn were the next successors of the Prophet. It is believed that Ḥasan was poisoned by his enemies. Ḥusayn was killed by his opponents in a battle near Karbala in C.E. 680.

6. Referring to that symbolism common to religious literature in the Middle East, H. Ritter writes: "The use of this metaphorical language does not in itself constitute a poetical achievement, which only comes into being by the manner of application of these metaphors, their combination, contraposition and so on." See *History of Iranian Literature*, pp. 86. Many of the characteristics of the description of Fáṭimih in ta'ziyah and in Bahá'u'lláh's Tablet of the Holy Mariner, including feminine symbolism for the divine and repeating devotional refrains can also be observed in early and medieval Christian mysticism. See for example, Saint Methodius' *The Symposium*.

7. In the early Bábí period there are also instances of the believers chanting the verses of the Qur'an, and intoning hymns of thanksgiving in a chorus of voices. See Nabíl-i A'ẓam, *The Dawn-Breakers*, pp. 393, 632.

8. Bahá'u'lláh, *Kitáb-i Aqdas*, pp. 61, 74.

9. Underhill, *Mysticism*, p. 79. This practice is known as dhikr (meaning *remembrance*) and refers to the remembrance of God. It is referred to in numerous passages in the Qur'an. The Báb used the term to refer to himself. See Lawson "The Terms 'Remembrance' (dhikr) and 'Gate' (báb) in the Báb's Commentary on the Sura of Joseph," *Studies in the Bábí and Bahá'í Religions*, vol. 5, pp. 1–63. The Arabic word dhikr is derived from the same root from which "to mention" is also derived. See Qur'an 8:2, 45; 33:41. In this sense, remembering God is also connected with mentioning or reciting the name of God, a devotional practice central to life in the Sufi orders.

10. With regard to rhythmic language, Evelyn Underhill also speaks of the "peculiar rhythmical language of genuine mystic dialogue" (Underhill, *Mysticism*, p. 278) referring to the back-and-forth between two speakers, such as divine Wisdom (Sophia) and a seeker. She uses Suso's (1295–1366 C.E.) "Book of the Eternal Wisdom" as an example, which contains a dialogue between "eternal Wisdom" and an "impetuous soul," referred to as "the servant." This type of dialogue structure can be observed in Bahá'u'lláh's Ode of the Dove. For a discussion of this ode, see Juan Ricardo Cole's "Bahá'u'lláh and the Naqshbandí Sufis in Iraq," in *From Iran East and West: Studies in Bábí and Bahá'í History*, vol. 4, pp. 15–19.

11. See Bahá'u'lláh, *Kitáb-i Aqdas*, p. 26

12. Translations of the "Fire Tablet" and the "Long Healing Prayer" can be found in *Writings of Bahá'u'lláh*, pp. 695–708, *Bahá'í Prayers*, pp. 221–9, and *Prayers of Ecstasy*, pp. 99–106, 107–116.

13. See Bahá'u'lláh, *Tablets*, pp. 118–119; *Epistle*, 131–34, and *Prayers of Ecstasy*, pp. 127–32.

CHAPTER 3: THE INTERPRETATION OF THE TABLET

1. A good presentation of these traditions can be found in English in Al-Ṭabarī's, *Commentary on the Qur'an* 32–34, see also translator's introduction xxvii–xxix. Some discussion can also be found in Sachiko Murata's *The Tao of Islam*, pp. 226, 227, 244; and William C. Chittick's *The Sufi Path of Knowledge*, pp. 269, 272, 282.

2. Bahá'u'lláh, *Kitáb-i Aqdas*, pp. 57, 80–81, 221–2.

3. The original context of this discussion is not clear from the text, but it may have originated from a discussion of the Gunjishk in 'Aṭṭár's *Conference of the Birds*.

4. Bahá'u'lláh, *Seven Valleys*, p. 42.

5. Bahá'u'lláh, *Certitude*, p. 175.
6. See for example, Bahá'u'lláh, *Certitude*, pp. 26, 43, 82, 115, 127, 220, 255.
7. With regard to the importance of adhering to the religious commandments, Rúmí writes, "The Law is like a lamp: It shows the way. Without a lamp, you will not be able to go forward. When you enter the path, your going is the Way. And when you reach the goal, that is the Truth." (Rumí, see William C. Chittick, *The Sufi Path of Love*, p. 10)
8. Among the Bahá'ís this would refer to 'Abdu'l-Bahá and Shoghi Effendi. Their examples are very instructive. In most instances, 'Abdu'l-Bahá's interpretations are supported by reference to the Báb's and Bahá'u'lláh's writings, the Qur'an, the Bible or other religious texts and traditions. His comments on the account of Adam in the Book of Genesis illustrates many aspects of how such texts should be interpreted. From a purely rational point of view, he begins with a rejection of the literal reading of the narrative while affirming the spiritual value of the text. He states: "it contains divine mysteries and universal meanings, and it is capable of marvelous explanations. Only those who are initiated into mysteries, and those who are near the Court of the All-Powerful, are aware of these secrets. Hence these verses of the Bible have numerous meanings." ('Abdu'l-Bahá, *Some Answered Questions*, p. 123) In this example, even text long regarded as historical narrative is identified as symbolic. Following these comments, 'Abdu'l-Bahá then gave an interpretation of the Adam and Eve narrative and ended with this encouragement of individual interpretation, "This is one of the meanings of the biblical story of Adam. Reflect until you discover the others." ('Abdu'l-Bahá, *Some Answered Questions*, p. 126) Even though his interpretation is regarded as authoritative among Bahá'ís, he does not seek to limit Bahá'ís with it. He does not assert that it is the best, most important, or that it is even the most useful interpretation of Genesis for every seeker's questions. The possibility of multiple interpretations suggests that different interpretations might illuminate different questions in a more relevant way. Finally, his assertion that "only those who are initiated into mysteries, and those who are near the Court of the All-Powerful, are aware of these secrets," followed by his encouragement that others should seek out the other meanings in the text, indicates that the essential criteria for interpreting sacred texts are in no way limited to the Prophets, Imáms, or himself.
9. Many commentators interpret the text by way of other texts in order to make their interpretations appear authoritative. Bahá'ís, however, make a distinction between personal and authoritative interpretation. See Bahá'u'lláh, *Kitáb-i Aqdas*, pp. 221–2. The fact that individual interpretations are not authoritative mitigates the divisive effects of multiple interpretations.
10. Among the Shí'ah, the Imám would not need any such referential evidence to justify a particular interpretation. Similarly, in the Bahá'í community, any interpretation of the appointed successors, 'Abdu'l-Bahá and Shoghi Effendi, on account of their appointment, as well as their holiness, wisdom, and divine protection, would be regarded as authoritative and in no need of justification.
11. *The Koran Interpreted* 16:45, trans. Arberry, see also 21:7.
12. "We have sent down to thee the Remembrance that thou mayest make clear to mankind what was sent down to them; and so haply they may reflect." (*The Koran Interpreted* 16:45, 46, trans. Arberry) Manifestations of God, such as Moses, are referred to in the Qur'an as the Remembrance of of God. See Qur'an 21:49.

13. See for example, Bahá'u'lláh, *Certitude*, pp. 3–4, 47, 68–70, 91, 187, 192–200.
14. Bahá'u'lláh writes, "He [the seeker] must so cleanse his heart that no remnant of either love or hate may linger therein, lest that love blindly incline him to error, or that hate repel him away from the truth." (Bahá'u'lláh, *Certitude*, p. 192)
15. Matthew 26:21–25.
16. The ark of eternity represents the religious community and those teachings that form the basis of the religious community, such as the Torah in Judaism, or the Gospel in Christianity. In particular, it signifies those aspects of the religious teachings that keep the community united and at peace. In a Bahá'í sense, these teachings are known as the covenant of God, a covenant safeguarded by a series of written documents that form part of the sacred scriptures of the religious community. These documents include Bahá'u'lláh's Kitáb-i 'Ahd (Book of the Covenant) and 'Abdu'l-Bahá's Will and Testament. Although Shoghi Effendi appointed no successor and left no will, many of his writings—most notably *The Dispensation of Bahá'u'lláh*—have been understood as fulfilling the same function with regard to the question of succession. These documents provide an authoritative basis for the succession of leadership within the community. The Bahá'í community now elects various governing bodies as anticipated and outlined in Bahá'u'lláh's writings. The provisions of the Bahá'í covenant, in effect, make unity and the avoidance of schism intrinsic to Bahá'í self-definition.
17. Mírzá Yaḥyá did make himself the leader of some among the remaining Bábí community, but he had very few followers. The majority of the Bábís became Bahá'ís, who now number in the millions throughout the world. The fate of Mírzá Yaḥyá is outlined by Moojan Momen in his article, "The Cyprus Exiles" (1991).
18. The Persian word *riḍván* means *paradise*, the ultimate expression of which is the primal garden of paradise and eschatological celestial paradise.
19. This letter was translated by Shoghi Effendi while he was at Balliol college at Oxford, England, and shortly after published in the November 23, 1921 edition of *Star of the West*, an early Bahá'í periodical. 'Abdu'l-Bahá's message was probably addressed primarily to Bahá'ís in the East, as the Tablet of the Holy Mariner was not yet available to the Bahá'ís in the West who probably knew little if anything about it. It was after the passing of 'Abdu'l-Bahá, that the actual Tablet of the Holy Mariner was first translated by Shoghi Effendi into English and published in the May 17, 1922 edition of *Star of the West*.
20. The expression "Blessed Beauty" is a designation often used by 'Abdu'l-Bahá to refer to Bahá'u'lláh.
21. After the passing of 'Abdu'l-Bahá in 1921, many individuals opposed Shoghi Effendi, most notably 'Abdu'l-Bahá's longstanding rival and half-brother Muḥammad 'Alí. See Rabbani, Rúḥíyyih's biographical account of the life of Shoghi Effendi, *The Priceless Pearl*, pp. 49–54, 69–71, and 118–24.
22. Matthew 24:28, NEB.
23. Bahá'u'lláh, *Seven Valleys*, pp. 12–13, Qur'an 41:53.
24. Bahá'u'lláh, *Hidden Words*, Arabic, no. 66. "Nor hearts contain Me" refers to the actual Essence of God, as distinct from what is attributed to God, such as love, power, majesty, etc. The well-known tradition, "Neither My heavens nor My earth can contain Me, but the heart of My faithful servant contains Me" (see, e.g., Ibn Arabi, *The Wisdom of the Prophets*, p. 133, trans. Angela Culme-Seymour) refers to the realm of attributes.

Statements spoken from the point of view of God's voice, such as "minds cannot grasp Me nor hearts contain Me" should not be taken as a claim to be God on the part of the speaker. Bahá'u'lláh's book, *The Hidden Words* contains a series of such statements written from this point of view. The text was compiled in 1858 when Bahá'u'lláh was a follower of the Báb. He likens the contents to the inner essence of what had been revealed to the Prophets in past times (Bahá'u'lláh, *Hidden Words*, p. 3).

25. Rúmí, *Mathnawí*, Book III, 1251–3. 14; from Chittick's *The Sufi Path of Love*, p. 274
26. Underhill, *Mysticism*, pp. 125–148.
27. See, for example, the Arabic *Hidden Words*, numbers 6, 7, 9, 10, 11, 12, 13, 14, 20, 35, 36, 37, 41, 43, 44, 58, 59, 61, 63, 64, 69.
28. See Bahá'u'lláh, *Tablets*, pp. 77, 140; *Prayers and Meditations*, pp. 48; *Gleanings*, pp. 183.
29. See Sours, "Bahá'í Cosmological Symbolism and the Ecofeminist Critique" *The Journal of Bahá'í Studies*, vol. 7, no. 1. (1995) pp. 37–44.

CHAPTER 4: THE SYMBOLISM OF THE TABLET

1. Bahá'u'lláh's early work, the Haft Vádí (The Seven Valleys), for example, is based on the same structure of Farídu'd-Dín 'Aṭṭár's seven valleys found in *The Conference of the Birds*. This work also contains frequent quotes from Jalálu'd-Dín Rúmí's writings.
2. Describing the characteristics of Persian literature, Jan Rypka writes, "Several embellishments . . . enjoy great popularity, e.g. parallelism (*muvāzana*), but above all hyperbole (*mubālagha*) and a hyperbolic method of expression in general (*ighrāq*)." See *History of Iranian Literature*, p. 100.
3. Some of the symbols pre-date the Hebrew scriptures, such as the Maiden and the Tree of Life. But the form used in Bahá'u'lláh's writings reflects the distinctive monotheistic and moral character they attained in the Hebrew tradition.
4. This metaphor can be observed in the panegyric on the Jewish saint Eleazar recorded in the forth book of Maccabees: "Like an outstanding pilot, indeed, the reason of our father Eleazar, steering the vessel of piety on the sea of passions, through buffeted by the threats of the tyrant and swamped by the swelling waves of torture, in no way served the rudder of piety until he sailed into the haven of deathless victory." (4 Maccabees 7:1–3. See *The Old Testament Pseudepigrapha* 2:552. See also Ecclesiasticus 43:24, Mark 4:35–41.)
5. The Báb, *Selections*, pp. 125–6.
6. Bahá'u'lláh, *Certitude*, p. 3.
7. See for example, Jalálu'd-Dín Rúmí, *Mathnawí*, Book III, 1311.
8. See Bahá'u'lláh, *Epistle*, p. 139.
9. Mark 4:35–41.
10. The Báb, *Selections*, pp. 57–58.
11. See Bahá'u'lláh, *Epistle*, p. 139.
12. For a brief overview of hierarchal cosmology in Bahá'u'lláh's writings see Sours, "Bahá'í Cosmological Symbolism and the Ecofeminist Critique" *The Journal of Bahá'í Studies*, vol. 7, no. 1, pp. 23–56. For an interesting study of hierarchy and cosmological symbolism in Islam, see Seyyed Hossein Nasr's *An Introduction to Islamic Cosmological Doctrines*.
13. Genesis 3:24.
14. Exodus 22.
15. Bahá'u'lláh, *Certitude*, pp. 79–80.

NOTES

16. See Peter J. Awn's *Satan's Tragedy and Redemption: Iblís in Sufi Psychology* for a detailed survey of how Satan (Iblís) is used as symbol in Sufi thought. See also M. J. Kister's "Legends in tafsír and hadíth Literature: The Creation of Adam and Related Stories," in *Approaches to the History of the Interpretation of the Qur'an*, pp. 88–100. For a brief consideration of how the angel Gabriel is used as a theophanic symbol in Bahá'u'lláh's writings, see Sours "Immanence and Transcendence in Theophanic Symbolism" *The Journal of Bahá'í Studies*. vol. 5, no. 2, pp. 34–35.
17. Isaiah 13–14, *NJB*.
18. The Báb, *Selections*, p. 64, cf. Qur'an 2:32; 38:74–78.
19. Bahá'u'lláh, *Epistle*, p. 41
20. Bahá'u'lláh explains the divine claims of Jesus and others in the Book of Certitude. He writes, "Thus in moments in which these Essences of being were deeply immersed beneath the oceans of ancient and everlasting holiness, or when they soared to the loftiest summits of divine mysteries, they claimed their utterance to be the Voice of divinity, the Call of God Himself. Were the eye of discernment to be opened, it would recognize that in this very state, they have considered themselves utterly effaced and non-existent in the face of Him Who is the All-Pervading, the Incorruptible. Methinks, they have regarded themselves as utter nothingness, and deemed their mention in that Court an act of blasphemy. For the slightest whispering of self, within such a Court, is an evidence of self-assertion and independent existence. In the eyes of them that have attained unto that Court, such a suggestion is itself a grievous transgression. How much more grievous would it be, were aught else to be mentioned in that Presence, were man's heart, his tongue, his mind, or his soul, to be busied with anyone but the Well-Beloved, were his eyes to behold any countenance other than His beauty, were his ear to be inclined to any melody but His voice, and were his feet to tread any way but His way." (Bahá'u'lláh, *Certitude*, pp. 179–180) In a later work, he responds to a critics objections to his claims stating: "O Shaykh! This station is the station in which one dieth to himself and liveth in God. Divinity, whenever I mention it, indicateth My complete and absolute self-effacement. This is the station in which I have no control over mine own weal or woe nor over my life nor over my resurrection." (Bahá'u'lláh, *Epistle*, p. 41)
21. Even though Bahá'u'lláh said that humanity was entering an age of maturity and his writings often reflect a great optimism for the world's future, he nonetheless, wrote this revealing passage concerning the next Manifestation of God to appear after him: "I am not apprehensive for My own self . . . My fears are for Him Who will be sent down unto you after Me—Him Who will be invested with great sovereignty and mighty dominion." (Bahá'u'lláh, as quoted by Shoghi Effendi; see Shoghi Effendi, *World Order*, p. 117) In other writings Bahá'u'lláh indicates that this next Manifestation would not appear before the passing of a thousand years. Bahá'u'lláh's writes "ere the expiration of a full thousand years" no one can lay "claim to a Revelation direct from God." (Bahá'u'lláh, *Kitáb-i Aqdas*, p. 32; see also Shoghi Effendi, *World Order*, p. 132) Bahá'u'lláh is, however, not trying to cancel out the validity of individual mystical experiences, such as dreams, visions, etc., as such experiences are well known and common in the history of the Bahá'í community. Rather this statement appears aimed at those who would claim that they have received a command from God that others must follow, such as new commandments comparable to those of Moses' law.

22. Bahá'u'lláh writes, "The knowledge of Him, Who is the Origin of all things, and attainment unto Him, are impossible save through knowledge of, and attainment unto, these luminous Beings who proceed from the Sun of Truth. By attaining, therefore, to the presence of these holy Luminaries, the 'Presence of God' [*liqá'u'lláh*] Himself is attained. From their knowledge, the knowledge of God is revealed, and from the light of their countenance, the splendor of the Face of God [*wajhu'lláh*] is made manifest. Through the manifold attributes of these Essences of Detachment, Who are both the first and the last, the seen and the hidden, it is made evident that He Who is the Sun of Truth is 'the First and the Last, the Seen, and the Hidden.' Likewise the other lofty names and exalted attributes of God. Therefore, whosoever, and in whatever Dispensation, hath recognized and attained unto the presence of these glorious, these resplendent and most excellent Luminaries, hath verily attained unto the "Presence of God" Himself, and entered the city of eternal and immortal life. Attainment unto such presence is possible only in the Day of Resurrection, which is the Day of the rise of God Himself through His all-embracing Revelation. (Bahá'u'lláh, *Certitude*, pp. 142–3/ Persian *Kitáb-i Íqán*, pp. 110–11) Note the use of the plural "holy Luminaries," "Essences of Detachment," etc., in His explanation, which indicates that this truth is applicable not just to Himself. (Bahá'u'lláh, *Certitude*, p. 142) Referring to the Manifestations of God, Bahá'u'lláh writes that "they soar in the heaven of the divine presence" (Bahá'u'lláh, *Certitude*, p. 67) and that "whosoever, *and in whatever Dispensation*, hath recognized and attained unto the presence of these glorious, these resplendent and most excellent Luminaries, hath verily attained unto the "Presence of God" Himself, and entered the city of eternal and immortal life. (Bahá'u'lláh, *Certitude*, p. 143, emphasis added)

23. Bahá'u'lláh, *Certitude*, p. 177.

24. Bahá'u'lláh quotes a tradition that reports Muhammad as saying, "I am Adam, Noah, Moses, and Jesus." (Bahá'u'lláh, *Certitude*, p. 162) In various statements, the Báb and Bahá'u'lláh refer to Adam as the first prophet. This understanding is common in the Islamic world. See Bahá'u'lláh, *Certitude*, pp. 162, 244; the Báb, *Selections*, pp. 89, 126.

25. The Báb, *Selections*, p. 108.

26. Rúmí, *Mathnawí*, Book II, 3453–7. 14. Translation from Chittick's *The Sufi Path of Love*, p. 123. Chittick list Nicholson as a source, but the translation differs and is more fluid.

27. Bahá'u'lláh, *Seven Valleys*, p. 11.

28. Matthew 16:19.

29. In order to prevent schism within the Bahá'í community, Bahá'u'lláh made a distinction between individual interpretation and authoritative interpretation. Individuals are encouraged to investigate the truth for themselves and to arrive at their own informed understanding of scripture. But it is not permitted that they should insist that others accept their views as authoritative, that is, assert that others are obligated to follow or imitate their understanding. Bahá'u'lláh appointed his son, 'Abdu'l-Bahá, as the sole authoritative interpreter of his teachings. 'Abdu'l-Bahá later appointed Shoghi Effendi as his successor and gave him the same authority of interpretation. Since it is taught that scripture has many meanings, this distinction between individual and authoritative interpretation has not had the effect of creating a narrow view of Bahá'u'lláh's writings, but rather has made the natural multiplicity of views less harmful to the community's unity. See Bahá'u'lláh, *Kitáb-i Aqdas*, pp. 221–2.

30. Daniel 12:3, *NJB*.
31. See Matthew 24: 29 and Bahá'u'lláh, *Certitude*, pp. 24–79.
32. See Qur'an 15:18, 37:7–10, 72:8–9.
33. See Schimmel, *Anvari's Divan: A Pocket Book for Akbar*, p. 63. "The image of stoning [cf. Qur'an 15:24] is preserved even on the cosmic plane, for when the faithful look up into the heavens at night and see shooting stars flash across the sky, they are witnessing the ceaseless battle between the spirit world and Iblīs. Every time Iblīs and his armies assault the heavens to secure a foothold in the land of his former glories, hosts of angels shower them with meteorites. Iblīs and his followers are driven once again to the lower regions of darkness." (See Peter J. Awn's *Satan's Tragedy and Redemption*, p. 38)
34. "His [Adam's] fall from Paradise was caused by his mixing too freely with the serpent—a warning for everyone who mixes with uncongenial and bad companions who keep him matterbound and jeopardize his spiritual pursuits." (Annemarie Schimmel, *The Triumphal Sun*, p. 250, see also, pp. 254–5) Bahá'u'lláh writes, "O Friend! In the garden of thy heart plant naught but the rose of love, and from the nightingale of affection and desire loosen not thy hold. Treasure the companionship of the righteous and eschew all fellowship with the ungodly." (Bahá'u'lláh, *Hidden Words*, Persian no. 3, p. 23)
35. Bahá'u'lláh, *Certitude*, pp. 193–4.
36. Qur'an 20:12–13.
37. Exodus 4:6–7, see Qur'an 7:108.
38. Exodus 33:18, *NJB*.
39. Exodus 33:18, *JPS*.
40. Exodus 33:19–22.
41. *The Koran Interpreted* 7:138–145, trans. Arberry.
42. Jewish legend contains this interesting story: "Shemhazai [the angel] beheld a girl whose name was Estirah. When he beheld her, he said, 'Listen to my request,' But she replied. 'I will not listen to thee until thou teachest me the name by the mention of which thou art enabled to ascend to heaven.' He forthwith taught her the Ineffable Name. She then uttered the Ineffable Name and thereby ascended to heaven. God said, 'Since she has departed from sin, go and set her among the stars'—it is she who shines brightly in the midst of the seven stars of Pleiades; for that she may always be remembered God fixed her among the Pleiades." (*The Chronicles of Jerahmeel*, p. 53)
43. Exodus 3:13, *JPS*.
44. Exodus 3:14, *JPS*.
45. John 8:56, *NJB*.
46. John 8:58, *NJB*.
47. Bahá'u'lláh, *Certitude*, p. 209.
48. The Báb, *Selections*, p. 74.
49. Ibid., p. 50.
50. Ibid., p. 72.
51. Bahá'u'lláh, *Tablets*, p. 242.
52. Bahá'u'lláh, *Epistle*, p. 112.
53. "In the thought of the ancient world a name does not merely distinguish a person from other persons, but is closely related to the nature of its bearer." (from O. S. Rankin's

word study "Name," see *A Theological Word Book of the Bible*, p. 157) See also Maimonides, *The Guide for the Perplexed* (chap. LXIV), pp. 95–6. In the Bahá'í writings, like the Bible and other scriptures, names and titles are sometimes used to distinguish one Manifestation of God from another. However, this is not their primary or exclusive role as noted above. In scripture, the primary role or function of the "name" is to identify and point out the spiritual reality that is present in the Manifestation. Because this same reality is present in them all, the names are universally applicable. "The personal character of God's revelation is expressed in the language of the Old Testament by the name of God. The name bears a fuller connotation than we associate with it in modern speech and probably comes nearer to our conception of person or personality. It is by the communication of his name that a personal being makes himself known to another. Thus when God makes known his name to men, it means that he makes himself personally known to them. Something resembling a formal introduction is recorded in Exod. 3:11–15 (cf. 6:2f), where the mysterious divine name is communicated to Moses. But the thought is more often of what the knowledge of the name of God means for those to whom it is given: they have access to his presence in prayer. This is particularly true of the temple in Jerusalem as the place of which God said, 'My name shall be there' (1 Kings 8:29). To know the name of God is to have a sure refuge (Ps. 9:9f). There is nothing in which the personality of God is more clearly expressed than in the fact that he has a name which he imparts to men as the means of establishing a personal relationship with them." (G. S. Hendry's word study of "Reveal," see *A Theological Word Book of the Bible* 200) See also Exodus 20:24, 23:21, Deuteronomy 12:11, Numbers 6:27, John 3:18, Acts 2:21, 1 Corinthians 1:13–15.

54. Bahá'u'lláh, *Prayers and Meditations*, p. 94.
55. Philippians 2:9–11, *NJB*.
56. Acts 4:12, *NJB*.
57. John 17:6, *NJB*. The *NKJV* reads, "I have manifested thy name."
58. Bahá'u'lláh, *Certitude*, p. 142.
59. Ibid., p. 179.
60. Ibid., p. 54.
61. Ibid., p. 11–2, emphasis added.
62. Luke 13:19, *NJB*.
63. Bahá'u'lláh, *Hidden Words*, pp. 18–19.
64. See Matthew 3:11. With regard to Jewish legend, Angelo S. Rappoport writes: "When Moses had passed the fire of Sandalphon he met the angel Rigyon who is really a fiery river issuing forth from underneath the Throne of Glory [cf. Daniel 7:10]. In this fiery stream the angels bathe every morning. Whenever the ministering angels appear before the Throne of Glory to be judged by the Lord of the Universe, they plunge into the fiery river of Rigyon and are rejuvenated. When the son of Amram had passed the fiery river of Rigyon, he met the angel Gallizur, who is also called Rasiel. It is he who listens to what is being proclaimed behind the veil before the Throne of Glory, and makes it known unto the world. And the prophet Elijah, standing upon the mount of Herob, hears the words proclaimed by the angel and announces the message to the world and to humanity." (Angelo S. Rappoport, *Ancient Israel: Myths and Legends*, pp. 52)
65. See for example, Bahá'u'lláh, *Seven Valleys* 11, *Certitude*, pp. 79, 194, 198, 205, 234. See also *Certitude*, p. 188.

NOTES

66. For similar imagery in Bahá'u'lláh's writings, see *Tablets*, p. 189, *cf.*, *Gleanings*, p. 156.
67. For an analysis of the parallels between the Maid of Heaven in Bahá'u'lláh's writings and the biblical wisdom literature, see Sours, "The Maid of Heaven, the Image of Sophia, and the Logos: Personifications of the Spirit of God in Scripture and Sacred Literature." *The Journal of Bahá'í Studies*. vol. 4, no. 1 (1991), pp. 47–65. Perhaps the most explicit connection appears in the sixth leaf of Words of Paradise (*Kalimát-i Firdawsiyyah*). See Bahá'u'lláh, *Tablets*, p. 66.
68. The Báb also identifies the Spirit of God within him as the Maid of Heaven: "O People of the earth! By the righteousness of the One true God, I am the Maid of Heaven begotten by the Spirit of Bahá, abiding within the Mansion hewn out of a mass of ruby, tender and vibrant; and in this mighty Paradise naught have I ever witnessed save that which proclaimeth the Remembrance of God by extolling the virtues of this Arabian Youth. Verily there is none other God but your Lord, the All-Merciful. Magnify ye, then, His station, for behold, He is poised in the midmost heart of the All Highest Paradise as the embodiment of the praise of God in the Tabernacle wherein His glorification is intoned." (The Báb, *Selections*, p. 54.)

    The words "begotten by the spirit of Bahá" (i.e., glory) find an interesting parallel in the Book of Wisdom, where Wisdom is described as "a breath of the power of God, pure emanation of the glory of the Almighty" who "renews the world, and generation after generation." (Wisdom 7:24–27, *NJB*) Correlations such as this suggest the importance of Jewish traditions and scriptures for an understanding of Bahá'u'lláh's writings. Jews, however, had come to exclude the Wisdom of Solomon from their canon, but it remained in the Catholic and Eastern canons. In the Muslim world various arguments had evolved, based according the Bahá'u'lláh, on a misinterpretation of the Qur'an, that Jews and Christians had corrupted their scriptures and that they no longer possessed the true Torah and Gospel. In his early and most important doctrinal work, Bahá'u'lláh tried to persuade people to give up this point of view and gain a greater appreciation of the Bible. In the Muslim world there was little direct knowledge of the Bible, apart from what was retold in the Qur'an and various popular historical books, but evidence from missionary accounts indicate the during the later part of the nineteenth century the Bábís and Bahá'í represented a change in this tendency. See Eugene Stock's *The History of the Church Missionary Society*, vol. III, p. 753. For attitudes toward the Hebrew Bible in the Islamic community, see Lazarus-Yafeh, *Intertwined Worlds*, p. 8. Concerning Bahá'u'lláh's defense of the Hebrew scriptures, *see* Bahá'u'lláh, *Certitude*, pp. 83–88. See also "Maimonides Replies" and "Jewish and Christian Tampering with Scriptures: A Muslim Critique" F. E. Peters, *Judaism, Christianity, and Islam*, pp. 194–5, 441–5; Robinson, *Christ in Islam and Christianity*, pp. 46–9. Concerning Bahá'u'lláh's defense of the Gospel, *see* Sours, *Without Syllable or Sound*, pp. 43–61.
69. Bahá'u'lláh as quoted by Shoghi Effendi. See Shoghi Effendi, *God Passes By*, pp. 101–2.
70. Bahá'u'lláh, *Tablets*, p. 66
71. Wisdom 7:27, *NJB*.
72. Qur'an 2:25, 3:15, 4:57; 37:48ff; 38:49–52; 43:70, 44:53–54; 52:20; 55:22, 23, 24, 56, 70, 72, 74, 76; 56:36, 72, 36; 78:34. These passages are from *The Holy Qur'an*, translation by Yusuf Ali. See also al-Ghazálí's, *The Remembrance of Death and the Afterlife*, pp. 244-6.
73. Qur'an 55:56.

74. Bahá'u'lláh, *Certitude*, pp. 70–71.
75. The Báb writes a soliloquy wherein the Maid of Heaven speaks about the Báb referring to him as "this Arabian Youth." See The Báb, *Selections*, p. 54. Like Bahá'u'lláh's reference to the ark and Sinai, his depiction of the Maid of Heaven referring to the "Arabian Youth" is another example of a corollary with the Báb's writings.
76. A 1955 letter written on behalf of Shoghi Effendi states, "In the Tablet of the Holy Mariner, the Youth means Bahá'u'lláh, Himself." *Unfolding Destiny*, p. 462.
77. See Bahá'u'lláh, *Tablets* 66 and Shoghi Effendi, *God Passes By*, pp. 101–2.
78. See Pelly, Scene 1 in *The Miracle Play of Hasan and Husain*. See also "Reprise: Joseph of the Seven Doors" in John Renard's *Seven Doors to Islam, Spirituality and the Religious Life of Muslims*, pp. 259–272 and Annemarie Schimmel's "Yúsuf in Mawláná Rumí's Poetry" in *The Legacy of Medæval Persian Sufism*, pp. 45–59.
79. Genesis 37:5–11, Qur'an 12:4–6.
80. Genesis 37.
81. See Shoghi Effendi, *God Passes By*, ch 10.
82. Genesis, ch. 41; Qur'an 40:34.
83. Bahá'u'lláh, *Certitude*, p. 178, see for example, also, pp. 4, 10, 13, 15, 17, 19.
84. See Shoghi Effendi, *God Passes By*, p. 185.
85. Bahá'u'lláh writes: "My sorrows are for those who have involved themselves in their corrupt passions, and claim to be associated with the Faith of God, the Gracious, the All-Praised. It behoveth the people of Bahá to die to the world and all that is therein, to be so detached from all earthly things that the inmates of Paradise may inhale from their garment the sweet smelling savor of sanctity . . ." (Bahá'u'lláh, *Gleanings*, pp. 100–1).
86. Qur'an 12:85
87. Qur'an 12:93
88. Bahá'u'lláh, *The Seven Valleys*, pp. 59–60. This passage is actually not in The Seven Valleys, but rather The Four Valleys, a separate work published currently together with The Seven Valleys.
89. Genesis 32:28, 43:6
90. See Qur'an 40:34, Bahá'u'lláh, *Certitude*, pp. 212–13.
91. Genesis 45:5–15, Qur'an 12:91–2, Bahá'u'lláh, *Kitáb-i Aqdas*, p. 87.
92. Bahá'u'lláh, *The Seven Valleys*, p. 9.
93. Matthew 14:34–6.

CHAPTER 5: REFLECTIONS ON THE TABLET

1. The invocation "He is the Gracious, the Well-Beloved!" serves to focus the attention on the divine attributes of God. Some invocations stress compassion, might or other qualities. The term "gracious" suggests God's indulgence with His servants, His compassion and mercy. The words "Well-Beloved" reflect an intimate and very personal vision of God, as one would have of a dearly-loved person.
2. The invocation "Glorified be my Lord, the All-Glorious!" occurs fifty-three times, whereas "Glorified be our Lord, the Most High!" occurs only following the final three verses. Both refrains use derivations of the word "Bahá," regarded as the Greatest Name in Bahá'í spirituality. The first refrain stresses God as "All-Glorious" a term used in scripture to indicate God's presence and immanence. The second refrain's use of the

words "Most High" stresses God's transcendence. The chorus of refrains therefore moves from emphasizing immanence to transcendence. Together they suggest the revealed and hidden nature of God.

3. Commenting on the hadíth "The parable of the Ship (Ark) of Noah: whoso shall cleave to it is saved, and whoso shall hold back from it is drowned," Jalálu'd-Dín Rúmí's writes:

> Of this account the Prophet said, "I am as the Ship (Ark) in the Flood of Time.
> I and my Companions are as the Ship of Noah: whoso clings (to us) will gain (spiritual) graces."
> When you are with the Shaykh [i.e., spiritual guide] you are far removed from wickedness: day and night you are a traveller and in a ship.
> You are under the protection of a life-giving spirit: you are asleep in the ship, you are going on the way.
> Do not break with the prophet of your days: do not rely on your own skill and footsteps.
> Lion though you are, you are self-conceited and in error and contemptible when you go on the way without a guide. (*Mathnawí*, Book IV, pp. 538–544, translated by Nicholson)

4. See Rúmí, *Mathnawí*, Book IV, 3357–9, Chittick's *The Sufi Path of Love*, p. 123.
5. Ibn 'Arabi, *Journey*, p. 55. "Elsewhere [*al-Futúhát* I, p. 150] he specifies that the difference between a prophet and a saint is that to a prophet the revelation brings legislation (*al-wahy bi l-tashrí'*) whereas in the case of a saint it is simply a confirmation of the authenticity of what has been brought by the prophet. In this way, the saint conforms to the Law not just by imitation (*taqlíd*) but as a result of an inner certainty ('*alā basīratin*)." (Abbas, *Quest*, p. 98)
6. Identification with past wisdom is important, as true wisdom acknowledges past wisdom. Bahá'u'lláh writes: "This is the changeless Faith of God, eternal in the past, eternal in the future." (Bahá'u'lláh, *Gleanings*, p. 136) Similarly, in the Bhagavad-Gítá Krishna both affirms the spiritual tradition of the past and identifies himself with it saying, "I instructed this imperishable science of yoga to the sun-god, Vivasván, and Vivasván instructed it to Manu, the father of mankind, and Manu in turn instructed it to Ikṣvāku. This supreme science was thus received through the chain of disciplic succession, and the saintly kings understood it in that way. But in course of time the succession was broken, and therefore the science as it is appears to be lost. That very ancient science of the relationship with the Supreme is today told by Me to you because you are My devotee as well as My friend and you can therefore understand the transcendental mystery of this science." (*Bhagavad-Gītā As It Is* 4:1–3, Trans. A. C. Bhaktivedanta Swami Prabhupāda) When Arjuna hears these words he is bewildered and responds: "The sun-god Vivasván is senior by birth to You. How am I to understand that in the beginning You instructed this science to him?" (*Bhagavad-Gītā As It Is* 4:4, Trans. A. C. Bhaktivedanta Swami Prabhupāda) This same point can be observed in Buddhist scripture. In the Mahapadana Suttanta, Buddha tells a group of monks about past "Buddhas Supreme." The monks are greatly amazed by this ability to have knowledge of the past. See T. W. and C. A. F. Rhys Davids, *Dialogues of the Buddha*, pp. 4–7.

7. Shoghi Effendi, *God Passes By*, p. 157
8. In Jewish legend fires of purification are associated with Moses' ascent to heaven. See note 64 in Chapter 4.
9. God is veiled because human beings are not capable of sustaining His full revelation, yet God is never totally veiled from the world, as creation is utterly dependent on God's grace. Ibn 'Arabi writes, "If He were to be veiled from the world for the blink of an eye, the world would vanish at one stroke; it only remains through His preserving and watching over it. However, His appearance in His light is so intense that it overpowers our perceptions, so that we call His manifestation a veil." (Ibn 'Arabi, *Journey*, pp. 25–6, see also p. 59) "Many a Persian poet compared poetry to a veiled bride, and Hafiz praised himself as a bridegroom peerless in his unveiling of that bride. Rúmí used a similar comparison, but invited the reader to unveil the beautiful maiden, to raise or cleave the curtain of her curls. . ." (Bürgel, *Poetry and Mysticism in Islam*, p. 45)
10. Jesus for example proclaims, "I have manifested Your name to the men whom You have given Me out of the world." (John 17:6, *NKJV*) See also, Bahá'u'lláh, *Tablets*, p. 182, *Epistle*, p. 97, and The Báb, *Selections*, p. 64.
11. Bahá'u'lláh, *Epistle*, p. 140.
12. Bahá'u'lláh, *Seven Valleys*, p. 17.
13. In the Bahá'í community, this is foremost the Báb and Bahá'u'lláh, and then Bahá'u'lláh's appointed successors 'Abdu'l-Bahá (1844–1921) and Shoghi Effendi (1897–1957), all of whom left many spiritual writings, letters of guidance, and prayers.
14. Bahá'u'lláh, *Seven Valleys*, p. 17.
15. "It is he [the angel Gallizur, who is also called Rasiel] who listens to what is being proclaimed behind the veil before the Throne of Glory, and makes it known unto the world. And the prophet Elijah, standing upon the mount of Herob, hears the words proclaimed by the angel and announces the message to the world and to humanity." (Angelo S. Rappoport, *Ancient Israel: Myths and Legends*, p. 52)
16. Bahá'u'lláh, *Seven Valleys*, p. 23
17. Ibn 'Arabi, *Journey*, p. 56.
18. Bahá'u'lláh, *Seven Valleys*, pp. 8, 42.
19. Ibid., p. 29.
20. See Bahá'u'lláh, *Certitude*, pp. 106–130.
21. Ibid., pp. 130–1.
22. See *The Holy Qur'an*, 55:56, 74; 55:70, 56:36; Yusuf Ali's trans.
23. See Bahá'u'lláh, *Certitude*, pp. 70–71.

BIBLIOGRAPHY

'Abdu'l-Bahá. *The Promulgation of Universal Peace: Talks Delivered by 'Abdu'l-Bahá During His Visit to the United States and Canada in 1912.* Comp. Howard MacNutt. Wilmette, Ill.: Bahá'í Publishing Trust, 1982.

———. *The Secret of Divine Civilization.* 3d ed. Trans. Marzieh Gail and 'Alí-Kuli Khan. Wilmette, Ill.: Bahá'í Publishing Trust, 1975.

———. *Selections from the Writings of 'Abdu'l-Bahá.* Comp. Research Department of the Universal House of Justice, trans. Marzieh Gail and a Committee at the Bahá'í World Centre. Haifa, Israel: Bahá'í World Centre, 1982.

———. *Some Answered Questions.* Rev. ed. Comp. and trans. Laura Clifford Barney. London: Bahá'í Publishing Trust, 1981.

———. *The Will and Testament of 'Abdu'l-Bahá.* Wilmette, Ill.: Bahá'í Publishing Trust, 1971.

Addas, Claude. *Quest for the Red Sulfur: The Life of Ibn 'Arabī.* Trans. Peter Kingsley. Cambridge, Islamic Text Society, 1993.

Awn. Peter J. *Satan's Tragedy and Redemption: Iblīs in Sufi Psychology.* Leiden, Netherlands: E. J. Brill, 1983.

A'zam, Nabíl-i. (Muhammad-i Zarandí). *The Dawn-Breakers, Nabíl's Narrative of the Early Days of the Bahá'í Revelation.* Wilmette, Ill.: Bahá'í Publishing Trust, 1974.

Báb, The. *Selections from the Writings of The Báb.* Comp. by the Research Department of the Universal House of Justice, trans. Habib Taherzadeh and a Committee at the Bahá'í World Centre. Haifa, Israel: Bahá'í World Centre, 1976.

Bahá'í Prayers, A Selection of Prayers Revealed by Bahá'u'lláh, the Báb, and 'Abdu'l-Bahá. Wilmette, Ill.: Bahá'í Publishing Trust, 1991.

Bahá'í prayers for Women: Selections from the Writings of Bahá'u'lláh, the Báb, 'Abdu'l-Bahá, and the Greatest Holy Leaf. Los Angeles: Kalimat Press, 2000.

Baha'i Scriptures: Selections from the Utterances of Baha'u'llah and Abdul Baha. Edited by Horace Holley. New York: Brentano's Publishers 1923.

Bahá'u'lláh. *The Book of Certitude (Kitáb-i Íqán).* 3d ed. Trans. Shoghi Effendi. Wilmette, Ill.: Bahá'í Publishing Trust, 1974.

———. *Epistle to the Son of the Wolf.* 3d ed. Trans. Shoghi Effendi. Wilmette, Ill.: Bahá'í Publishing Trust, 1976.

———. *Gleanings from the Writings of Bahá'u'lláh.* 2d ed. Trans. Shoghi Effendi. Wilmette, Ill.: Bahá'í Publishing Trust, 1956.

———. *The Hidden Words of Bahá'u'lláh.* Trans. Shoghi Effendi. Wilmette, Ill.: Bahá'í Publishing Trust, 1985.

———. *Kitáb-i Aqdas.* Bahá'í World Centre, Haifa, Israel, 1992.

———. *Kitáb-i Íqán* (Persian). Hofhein-Langenhain, Germany: Bahá'í-Verlag, 1980.

———. *The Seven Valleys and The Four Valleys of Bahá'u'lláh.* Rev. translation. Trans. Ali Kuli Khan. Wilmette, Ill.: Bahá'í Publishing Trust, 1967.

———. *Prayers and Meditations of Bahá'u'lláh.* 2d ed. Trans. Shoghi Effendi. Wilmette, Ill.: Bahá'í Publishing Trust, 1956.

———. *The Proclamation of Bahá'u'lláh.* Haifa, Israel: Bahá'í World Centre, 1972.

———. *Tablets of Bahá'u'lláh revealed after the Kitáb-i Aqdas.* Comp. Research Department of the Universal House of Justice, trans. Habib Taherzadeh and a Committee at the Bahá'í World Centre. Haifa, Israel: Bahá'í World Centre, 1978.

Balyuzi, H. M. *Bahá'u'lláh: King of Glory.* Oxford: George Ronald, 1980.

———. *Eminent Bahá'ís in the Time of Bahá'u'lláh.* Oxford: George Ronald, 1985.

Bhagavad-Gītā As It Is. Trans. and commentary by A. C. Bhaktivedanta Swami Prabhupāda. Los Angeles: Bhaktivendanta Book Trust, 1990.

Bible, The Holy: New King James Version. Nashville, Tenn.: Thomas Nelson, 1982.

Bible, New Jerusalem. New York: Doubleday, 1985.

Chittick, William C. *The Sufi Path of Knowledge.* Albany: State University of New York Press, 1989.

———. *The Sufi Path of Love.* Albany: State University of New York Press, 1983.

The Chronicles of Jerahmeel. Translated by M. Gaster. 1899. New York: Ktav Publishing House, Inc., 1971.

Cole, Juan Ricardo. "Bahá'u'lláh and the Naqshbandí Sufis in Iraq" *From Iran East and West: Studies in Bábí and Bahá'í History.* 4:1–28 Edited by Juan R. Cole and Moojan Momen. Los Angeles: Kalimát Press, 1984.

———. "Bahá'u'lláh's 'Súrah of the Companions': An Early Edirne Tablet of Declaration (c. 1864)." *Bahā'ī Studies Bulletin.* Vol. 5, no. 3, pp. 4–30, June 1991.

BIBLIOGRAPHY

Dialogues of the Buddha. Vol. II. Trans. T. W. and C. A. F. Rhys Davids. London: Luzac & Company Ltd., 1971.

Dictionary of the Bible, A. Vol. I. Edited by James Hastings. 1898. Reprint, Peabody, Mass.: Hendrickson, 1988.

Elwell. *Evangelical Dictionary of Theology.* Grand Rapids, Mich.: Baker Book House, 1987.

Erickson, Millard J. *Christian Theology.* Grand Rapids, Mich.: Baker Book House, 1985.

al-Ghazālī, Abū Ḥāmid Muhammad ibn Muhammad. *The Remembrance of Death and the Afterlife.* Cambridge: The Islamic Text Society, 1989.

History of Iranian Literature. Edited by Jan Rypka. Dordrecht, Holland: D. Reidel Publishing Company, 1968.

Jámí, Mulláná Abdulrahmán. *The Book of Joseph and Zuleikha.* Trans. by Alexander Rogers. London: David Nutt, 1892.

Koran, The. Trans. Rodwell. 1909. Reprint, London: Everyman's Library, 1971.

Korân, The. Trans. George Sale. 1734. London: Frederick Warne and Co., Ltd., (n. d.).

Koran Interpreted, The. Trans. A. J. Arberry. New York: MacMillan Co., 1970.

Lambden, Stephen N. "The Sinaitic Mysteries: Notes on Moses/Sinai Motifs in Bábí and Bahá'í Scripture." Vol. 5. *Studies in the Bábí and Bahá'í Religions: Studies in Honor of the Late Hasan M. Balyuzi.* Ed. by Moojan Momen. Los Angeles: Kalimát Press, 1988.

———. "Some Notes on Bahá'u'lláh's Gradually Evolving Claims of the Adrianople/Edirne Period." *Bahá'í Studies Bulletin.* Vol. 5, no. 3, June 1991, pp. 75–83.

Lawson, B. Todd. "The Terms 'Remembrance' (*dhikr*) and 'Gate' (*báb*) in the Báb's Commentary on the Sura of Joseph." *Studies in the Bábí and Bahá'í Religions,* vol. 5: *Studies in Honor of the Late Hasan M. Balyuzi.* Ed. by Moojan Momen. Los Angeles: Kalimát Press, 1988.

Lazarus-Yafeh, Hava. *Intertwined Worlds: Medieval Islam and Bible Criticism.* Princeton University Press, 1992.

Legacy of Mediæval Persian Sufism, The. Edited by Leonard Lewisohn. London, Khaniqahi Nimatullahi Publications, 1992.

Lights of Guidance: A Bahá'í Reference File. 2d rev. ed. Comp. Helen Hornby. New Delhi: Bahá'í Publishing Trust, 1988.

Maimonides, Moses. *The Guide for the Perplexed.* Trans. and edited by by Shlomo Pines. Chicago, Ill.: University of Chicago Press, 1963.

Methodius, Saint. *The Symposium: A Treatise on Chastity.* Translated and annotated by Herbert Musurillo. Westminster, Md: The Newman Press, 1958.

Momen, Moojan. "The Cyprus Exiles." *Bahá'í Studies Bulletin.* Vol. 5, no. 3 (June, 1991), pp. 84–115.

Muller, Richard A. *Dictionary of Latin and Greek Theological Terms.* Grand Rapids, Mich.: Baker Book House, 1989.

Murata, Sachiko. *The Tao of Islam*. Albany: State University of New York Press, 1992.

Nasr, Seyyed Hossein. *An Introduction to Islamic Cosmological Doctrines*. Albany: State University of New York Press, 1993.

New Bible Dictionary. 2d ed. Ed. J. D. Douglas. Wheaton, Ill.: Tyndale House Publishers Inc., 1982.

The Old Testament Pseudepigrapha. Vol. 2. Ed. by James H. Charlesworth. Garden City, New York: Doubleday & Company, Inc., 1985.

Pelly, Colonel Sir Lewis. *The Miracle Play of Hasan and Husain. Collected from oral tradition*. Vols. I and II. Rev. with explanatory notes by Arthur N. Wollaston. London: Wm. H. Allan and Co., 1879.

Peters, F. E. *Judaism, Christianity, and Islam: The Classical Texts and Their Interpretation*. Princeton University Press, 1990.

Prayers of Ecstasy: Selections from the Bahá'í Sacred Writing. Los Angeles: Kalimat Press, 2001.

Qur'an, The Holy. 2d ed. Trans. Yusuf Ali. American Trust Publications for the Muslim Students' Association, 1977.

Rabbani, Rúhiyyih. *The Priceless Pearl*. London: Bahá'í Publishing Trust, 1969.

Rappoport, Angelo S. *Ancient Israel: Myths and Legends*. Vol. 1. London: Senate, an imprint of Studio Editions, Ltd., 1995.

A Reader on Islam: Passages from Standard Arabic Writings Illustrative of the Beliefs and Practices of Muslims. Ed. Arthur Jeffery. New York: Arno Press, 1980.

Robinson, Neal. *Christ in Islam and Christianity*. Albany: State University of New York Press, 1991.

Rúmí, Jaláu'ddín. *The Mathnawí*. Vols. I–VI. Translated by Reynold A. Nicholson. Cambridge University Press, 1982.

Schimmel, Annemarie. *Anvari's Divan: A Pocket Book for Akbar*. New York: Metropolitan Museum of Art, 1983.

Shoghi Effendi. *God Passes By*. Wilmette, Ill.: Bahá'í Publishing Trust, 1974.

———. *The Unfolding Destiny of the British Bahá'í Community: Messages from the Guardian of the Bahá'í Faith to the Bahá'ís of the British Isles*. London: Bahá'í Publishing Trust, 1981.

———. *The World Order of Bahá'u'lláh*. 2d ed. Wilmette, Ill.: Bahá'í Publishing Trust, 1974.

Sours, Michael W. "Bahá'í Cosmological Symbolism and the Ecofeminist Critique" *The Journal of Bahá'í Studies*. Vol. 7, no. 1 (1995) pp. 23–56.

———. "Immanence and Transcendence in Theophanic Symbolism" *The Journal of Bahá'í Studies*. Vol. 5, no. 2 (1992) pp. 13–56.

———. "The Maid of Heaven, the Image of Sophia, and the Logos: Personifications of the Spirit of God in Scripture and Sacred Literature." *The Journal of Bahá'í Studies*. Vol. 4, no. 1. (1991) pp. 47–65.

———. *Without Syllable or Sound: The World's Sacred Scriptures in the Bahá'í Faith*. Los Angeles: Kalimát Press, 2000.

Star of the West. Vol. XII, no. 14 (November 23, 1921). Chicago, Ill.: Bahai News Service, 1921. Facsimile reprint: *Star of the West*. Vol. 7 (March 1921–November 1922). Oxford: George Ronald, 1984.

———. Vol. XIII, no. 4 (May 17, 1922). Chicago, Ill.: Bahai News Service, 1922. Facsimile reprint: *Star of the West*. Vol. 7 (March 1921–November 1922). Oxford: George Ronald, 1984.

Stock, Eugene. *The History of the Church Missionary Society*. Vol. III. London: Church Missionary Society, 1899.

Al-Ṭabarī. *Commentary on the Qur'ān, The*. Vol. I. Trans. J. Cooper. Oxford University Press, 1989.

Tanakh: The Holy Scriptures (The New Jewish Publication Society Translation According to the Traditional Hebrew Text). Philadelphia, Penn.: The Jewish Publication Society, 1985.

Ta'ziyeh: Ritual and Drama in Iran. Ed. by Peter J. Chelkowski. New York University Press and Soroush Press, 1979.

Theological Dictionary of the New Testament. Vol. I. Ed. Gerhard Kittel. Grand Rapids, Mich.: Wm. B. Eerdman's Publishing Company, 1977.

Theological Word Book of the Bible, A. Ed. Alan Richardson. New York: MacMillan Publishing Co., 1978.

Theological Wordbook of the Old Testament. Vol. 1. Edited by R. Laird Harris; Associate editors, Gleason L. Archer, Jr. and Bruce K. Waltke. Chicago, Ill.: Moody Press, 1980.

Vine, W. E. *Vine's Expository Dictionary of Biblical Words*. Rev. ed. Nashville: Thomas Nelson, 1985.

Vincent, Marvin R. *Vincent's Word Studies of the New Testament*. Vol. 1. 2d. ed. 1888. Reprint. Peabody, Mass.: Hendrickson (n. d.).

Wellspring of Guidance, Messages from the Universal House of Justice: 1963–1968. Rev. ed. Wilmette, Ill.: Bahá'í Publishing Trust, 1976.